THE ARCHAEOASTRONOMY OF A FEW

MEGALITHIC SITES OF JHARKHAND

THE ARCHAEOASTRONOMY OF A FEW MEGALITHIC SITES OF JHARKHAND

SUBHASHIS DAS

NIYOGI
BOOKS

Published by

NIYOGI BOOKS

Block D, Building No. 77,
Okhla Industrial Area, Phase-I,
New Delhi-110 020, INDIA
Tel: 91-11-26816301, 26818960
Email: niyogibooks@gmail.com
Website: www.niyogibooksindia.com

Editor: Siddhartha Banerjee
Design: Shashi Bhushan Prasad

ISBN: 978-93-86906-16-8
Publication: 2018

Printed at: Niyogi Offset Pvt. Ltd., New Delhi, India

... to the unknown megalith-makers

“Every man carries with him unconsciously the memory of ancient civilisations. Similarly, the rock is a fragment of the world’s memory.

—Carl Gustav Jung

CONTENTS

PREFACE

Migration of the various Proto-Australoid Kolarian Mundari tribes into India commenced in the early part of the second millennium BC. They trekked to India from Sumer/Chaldea via the various mountain passes along the North-West Frontier, bringing with them their culture, religion, and a technology of megalith-making applying astronomy and mathematics.

Numerous sources indicate the presence of various Kolarian and Dravidian Kurukh/Kudukh-speaking tribes in the Harappa region of what is now Pakistan and western India. Several Adivasis, such as the Gond, Oraon, Santal, et al., have for long claimed to be the authors of the Indus Valley Civilisation. Their claim also finds resonance in their folktales and songs. The Santal still chant of the glory of 'Sinjho Nai', the name used by them to refer to the river Sindhu or Indus. Recorded in Santal tradition are distinct events believed to have taken place during the course of the tribe's prolonged stay in the Indus region. If that were the case, a variety of Mundari languages, too, must have been ubiquitous in the region. Southworth staunchly believed in the prevalence of a para-Munda speech in the area (Southworth 2005, 328–329). Michael Witzel reckons that the Indus area may have been a multilingual and multi-ethnic region with a prevalent para-Mundari language among others. Jaidev Baghel, a distinguished Dokra craftsman from Chhattisgarh and a Kolarian tribal, also maintains that tribal Dokra craftsmanship had widely proliferated the Indus region.

These non-Aryan tribals subsequently moved from the Indus and other provinces in the west and gradually spread to regions of northern, central, and eastern India. The preponderance of Mundari names for towns, villages, rivers, and hills across these regions alludes to a time in the country's past that once was predominantly tribal, prior to her Aryanisation. Such names also validate the Mundari and Dravidian Kurukh/Kudukh-speaking people's tales of migration into India through these tracks, wherein they named villages, hills, rivers, etc. in their respective languages wherever they dwelled during prehistory, many of which still remain in use. The name Kurukshetra, for instance, implies that the place was the *kshetra* or region of Kurukh-speaking tribes.

The megaliths at Asota in Pakistan and Burzahom in Indian Kashmir are seemingly enduring testimonials of the eastward migration of megalithic tribes during prehistory. While a few ancient megaliths are extant in localities with tribal populations, others, such as the one at Deosa in Rajasthan, have been demolished and their stones appropriated for mundane domestic purposes.

That tribals are a cultured lot with their own societal constructs is not acknowledged by the populace at large. Aryan attitudes and texts, not having cared to delve deeper into tribal culture, consider tribalism barbaric and uncivilised. Regardless of such blatant misinformation, the tribals, who although do not boast of any script or written literature, preserve a fine history of their community in the form of folklore and tradition, and by way of archaeological relics known as megaliths. Such folklore, spurned both by historians and scholars as inconsequential, yet deemed by many to be oral history, is indeed as noteworthy as any written text. The populace at large should be apprised that Adivasi culture is indeed very rich and prosperous, with their own forms of democratic governance, social set-up, medicine, music, arts and crafts, religion, and mathematics and astronomy.

Although India is a treasure trove of megaliths, as is evident from the presence of these ancient monuments across the country, from Kashmir to Kerala and from Tripura to Gujarat, they have not been paid much heed by historians and archaeologists as being significant relics of our prehistory.

The surface positioning of prehistoric megalithic complexes reveal that many of them were consciously established employing mathematical principles. These then serve as confirmation of the fact that these ancient unknown and unnamed people were not a lesser set of beings, as is commonly assumed, but were persons adept in simple mathematics and astronomy, preceding Aryan mathematician-astronomers like Baudhayana, Aryabhata, Varahamihira, et al. by thousands of years.

AN OVERVIEW

Colin Mackenzie is generally regarded as the first person to study and draw megaliths in India, having documented megalithic burials in South India (Paddayya 1997, 38). However, it is J. Babington who should be credited with having brought to attention the first megalithic site in India—in 1823, he excavated a megalith at Chattaparamba in the Malabar region of Kerala (Babington 1823). In 1853, Captain Meadows Taylor excavated a megalithic burial site in Sorepur (Das 2009). J.H. Rivett-Carnac excavated the Junapani megaliths near Nagpur in 1870 and 1879. In 1915, Alexander Rea opened the megaliths of Perumbair and Adichanallur in Tamil Nadu. J.H. Hutton excavated a few megaliths in Assam in 1922 (Thapar and Sharma 1994, 1). Sadly, no information about these excavations is now available. Consequently, it was during the excavation of the Brahmagiri megaliths that a chronology was fixed for these monuments. A number of megalithic monuments have since been excavated across the subcontinent, their precise documentation adding considerably to our understanding of these tombs and their makers. Later, in 1949, Krishnaswami pioneered the classification of megaliths in India (Rao 1972). But it was Moorti who categorised megaliths into sepulchral or burial and non-sepulchral or memorial forms (Moorti 1994).

It is not known for certain who the first person to discover the first megalith in the state of Jharkhand was. Col. Dalton was perhaps among the first to document the megaliths of the state. He was apprised by one T.F. Pepe about the Munda burial ground at Chokahatu in the early 1870s; Col. Dalton subsequently brought to light Chokahatu and various other megalithic sites of the state (Dalton 1872, 115). Jharkhand shall forever remain indebted to both Col. Dalton and T.F. Pepe for bringing the megaliths of the state to public attention.

However, this book is not on archaeology per se but on the archaeoastronomy or astroarchaeology of a few megalithic sites of Jharkhand. Archaeoastronomy is the study of the positioning of structures, be it ancient temples, churches, or prehistoric megaliths, in alignment with the rising sun, the moon, or certain stars as seen on specific days (Earis 2011, 3).

The temples of Hindus, Buddhists, and Jainas can be seen oriented towards the rising sun, i.e. due east or as seen on other significant days. Applied astronomy and geometry have also been found in the cities of the Indus valley. R.S. Bisht, former joint director general of the Archaeological Survey of India, ascertained that several ancient cities in the Indus valley such as

Dholavira were arranged according to principles of mathematics and astronomy (Bisht 1997). That geometry was applied in the construction of Harappan cities was also determined by Michel Danino, a freelance researcher on the Indus valley (Danino 2004-05). Even the bricks in these cities were found to manifest specific ratios.

A study of the many ancient megaliths (henceforth many a time referred to as temples) in the state of Jharkhand by the author revealed alluring alignments, both with hills in the landscape and the directions of sunrise and sunset on equinoxes and solstices. The study also showed that, apart from astronomy, the arrangement of stones within these astronomical temples of the state also adhere to geometry. That the ancient tribals were aware of such intricate sciences is testified by many of these prehistoric megalithic temples, which stand in stark contradiction to the established belief that astronomy and mathematics are the creations of Brahmanical scholars like Aryabhata and Varahamihira, and evolved many centuries later.

These were the times of the fertility cults of the ubiquitous Great Goddesses in India. Megaliths, as an upshot of contemporary research, are held as products of this once widespread but now obsolete cult. However, in rural areas, many tribal and Dalit communities still perform ritualistic worship to these ancient stones and burials.

In Jharkhand, despite there being a large cache of megaliths, excavation of these monuments has not been undertaken till date. As a result, there is not much cognisance regarding their grave yields or the antiquity of these monuments. Road constructions have destroyed many a megalith, revealing buried pots containing ash, iron or copper implements, bone fragments, stone/metal arrowheads, and even coins in the process. Such discoveries indicate that pot burials were the typical mode of entombment in these megaliths. Nevertheless, future excavations are bound to unearth other burial forms, which may have been prevalent during prehistory, amongst the multiplicity of megaliths the state contains.

Archaeologists ascribe the megaliths of Jharkhand to the Iron Age—an assertion based on mere speculation, articulated without conducting a single excavation. One megalithic site, at Pathalgada in Chatra district, which was completely ruined in the process of road-making, revealed to the author and his team prehistoric pots comprising only copper remains. This discovery could be instrumental in pushing back the dates of Jharkhand megaliths to the Chalcolithic period. However, a thorough investigation is essential to arrive at a verifiable conclusion.

Fundamentally, the megaliths of Jharkhand are burial sites or memorials for the dead, raised by the tribals of the state since the Neolithic or metal ages. Nonetheless, the research of the author on the megaliths of the state, conducted over a span of about 20 years, has revealed to him some of the most extraordinary ancient astronomical stone temples, constructed in antiquity for astronomical purposes by tribals with at least a basic understanding of geometry and horizon astronomy.

HILLS ARE SACRED

To present-day tribals of Jharkhand, hills are manifestations of the highly venerated Marang Buru. However, during ancient times, hills were revered both as the breasts and the vulva of the omnipresent Mother Goddess; these were times when a large section of the world believed in the now almost obsolete fertility cults. A number of rites and customs of this cult percolated over time both into the Hindu and tribal faiths.

Hills are identified today in their male and female forms as *pahad* (male hill) and *pahadi* (female hill) (Das 2009). To revere hills as *pahadi* is a custom that has emerged from the fecundity cults of antiquity, when all hills were deemed mother deities or goddesses. It was an ancient convention, observed by Mother tribes across the prehistoric world (including India)—to view hills with specific contours as pregnant, recumbent Great Goddesses (Cope 1998) (Plate 1). It is to such hills that many megaliths have been found to be aligned (Das 2009).

Plate 1

To the Proto-Australoid Kolarian and the Dravidian Kudukh-speaking tribes, hills were known as *buru*. Aligning megaliths to Mother hills on the horizon elevated these burial-shrines to the stature of Mother temples. Although menhirs in Jharkhand are called *birdiri, birkhod,* or *birkhol,* it is perhaps because of such alignments to the *burus* or hills in the landscape that they also came to be known as *burudiri*.

Many a time one may find that a few of the stones in a megalithic complex are not aligned with any hills. If that be the case, it

is probably because they are oriented towards equinoctial and solstitial sunrises and sunsets (Earis 2011).

SELECTION OF SITE

Our survey of the ancient megalithic sites in Jharkhand revealed that these stone temples were not randomly located. Hills were a necessity for the establishment of a megalithic site, a dolmen,

PLATE 1 *Juljul* pahadi, *Hazaribagh*

or even a single menhir so that the stones may be coupled to the hills in the landscape by way of alignments.

The ancient megalithic astronomer-priests thus opted for circular landscapes with hills in the opposite horizons and where an intersectional point could be created by way of alignments with these hills. The intersection points were held as places of sacred prominence and it is at such consecrated locations that prehistoric megaliths have been found positioned.

Such intersections by way of alignments to the hills, on which ancient megaliths can be seen to have been placed, are also reckoned as sacred omphalos, and, in the process, a 'cross within a circle'-type design is created on the ground (Drawings 2 and 4). Incidentally, the cross-within-a-circle is an exceedingly revered symbol, found at several prehistoric cave art sites and megalithic structures across the world, and can yet be seen in use in several Hindu ceremonies.

The hills along with the landscape thus form the outer precincts of an ancient megalithic burial-temple and the temple is incomplete without them (Cope 1998, 9).

MEGALITHS OF JHARKHAND

Jharkhand is one of the few places in the world where megalith-making continues unremittingly among a few tribes since the Chalcolithic era, or perhaps from an even earlier age.

For these tribes, their megaliths—*sasandiris*, *birdiris*, and *pathalgadas*—are vestiges of paramount significance. A story goes that when the British insisted that the Adivasi peoples of Jharkhand show them ownership documents of their villages, they declared they had none. However, to prove to the British that their villages had existed for thousands of years, they showed them the megalithic burial grounds of their villages, referred to colloquially as *hargarhi, harsali, jangarha,* etc.

These ancient burial grounds housed prehistoric megaliths raised by the villagers in honour of their departed ancestors. It is believed that the antiquity of the ancestral stones inside the *hargarhi*s had dumbfounded the foreigners; the ancient burial grounds presented indubitable evidence that the villages had existed since antiquity. The British were further stunned to discover that the tribals, who had been erecting funerary monuments for the deceased since time immemorial, were still doing so.

But not all megaliths, be it a lone monument, a cluster, or a complex, were established for cinerary purposes. The following text explores the various rationales behind these enigmatic structures in stone.

AS SEPULCHRAL MONUMENTS AND MEMORIALS OF THE DEAD

Jharkhand is a state of ongoing megalithism, and, as such, is a veritable treasure trove of megaliths. The state is home to an assortment of megalithic architecture with variation from one region to another (Das 2008, 181). The standard dolmen or the single-slab-type individualistic burials, referred to as *sasandiri*s in Austric speech, can be found in all the burial grounds of the state's tribal villages. These burial grounds, known alternatively as *hargarhi, harsali, jangarha,* etc. in the tribal vernacular, in turn exist in each tribal village.

Individual vertical or inclined stones planted in the ground are called menhirs, and are referred to as *birdiri*s or *burudiri*s in the Austric speech. These menhirs stand as memorials inside a particular *hargarhi* or even outside as boundary markers of a village, known consequently as *simana diri*. Several *hargarhi*s of the state are devoid of *sasandiri* dolmens but feature *birdiri* menhirs; a few, such as Bayen, Punkri Burwadih, Banadag, et al., even comprise stone circles.

Currently, tribes such as the Asur, Oraon, Munda, and Ho still construct megalithic tombs for their dead. Although the Santal are not known to be a tribe with a megalithic tradition, they do occasionally build cairns with grits of stones on their dead. The Bhumij and the Kasia, too, are known to have placed stone slabs on their dead. It is of course difficult to now ascertain which other tribe may have been megalithic in the disposal of their dead. The burial grounds can be seen positioned with *burus* or hills to the north and south. Many a time the burial grounds would be located adjacent to a North–South flowing river, on the banks of which the dead were cremated.

Although all the earlier mentioned megalithic tribes still erect *sasandiri*s on their dead, there exist architectural variances among these shrines in compliance with the traditions of the respective community. The Munda *sasandiri* is actually a burial dolmen comprising three, four, or six stone stands, on which rests a flat cap-stone (Plate 2). A *sasandiri* is essentially a vault of pots containing the bones and incinerated ash of the dead belonging to the same family (Koppers 1942, 186). Even in the absence of a stone vault, the pot holding the deceased's cremated bones is buried in the ground and a megalith raised on top of it. The Asur and Ho *sasandiri*s are essentially recumbent stone slabs under which cinerary pots are inserted. The Ho, however, build *sasandiri*s in the courtyards of their homes.

Plate 2

Plate 3

Plate 4

The architecture of the Oraon *sasandiri* is fundamentally different—they erect a *birdiri* adjacent to a customary *sasandiri* (Das 2014, 115). The structure resembles a large stone chair and is thus called a *kursi* (Dalton 1872). Presently, however, the architectural nuances having become diluted, a Munda can also be seen erecting a *sasandiri* similar to that of the Oraon's (Plate 4). Munda *birdiri* menhirs are tall and can be seen positioned in rows; Ho menhirs are slender and taller and are relatively newer.

The Santal are believed to be a non-megalithic tribe, but evidence shows that they did build stone cairns, mounds, and *sasandiri*s during their stay in Hazaribagh and Chatra. Their *sasandiri* is indeed quite different, wherein a larger menhir leans on a smaller standing stone. Seeing that this type of structure has no pre-existing archaeological name, the author has taken the liberty to dub it 'lean-support megalith' (Plate 3). The Santal do not build *sasandiri*s on their dead anymore; however, lean-support structures can still be seen in Santal villages, not as sepulchral monuments but as paddy-threshing structures. Nevertheless, the Santal still build cairns or burial mounds on their dead.

*Birdiri*s are erected as memorials of the departed, or even as commemoratives for significant events in a village or in a family.

PLATE 2 *A Munda* sasandiri *in the* hargarhi *of Chokahatu.*

PLATE 3 *A Santali 'lean-support'* sasandiri.

PLATE 4 *A modern-day Oraon-type Mundari* sasandiri.

Many megaliths in Jharkhand carry traces of black bitumen on the top, indicating a cinerary ritual; most megalithic burials and memorials reveal extensive customs. Many a time menhirs are even adorned with white clothes as a funerary ritual (Plate 4).

A *birdiri* could even be raised in the memory of a dead animal (Das 2009, 174). Jharkhand being among the most amazing megalithic states of the country, megalithism thrives here in many forms. In Ranchi district, I have seen a menhir raised in the memory of a dead baby elephant. I also heard a most fascinating and unusual legend surrounding a menhir in a village called Dehkel, located in the dense woods of Gumla district. The story goes that a tiger once fell in love with a belle from that village and impregnated her. When she eventually gave birth, it was found that the baby was not human but a tiger cub. The tiger toddler turned out to be a playful cub that the entire village adored. As the cub grew older, it began slaying the village's cattle stock for endurance. Helpless, the villagers killed the cub and raised a menhir on its dead remains.

Solitary menhirs, dolmens, cairn circles, and even oblongs have been spotted across the state of Jharkhand. The presence of such a wide array of ancient megalithic constructions may be ascribed to different tribes, the cause of death (Koppers 1942, 187), graves belonging to people of different genders or ages, etc. (Van Exem 1982). The contemporary megalithic tribes of the state only erect *sasandiri* and *birdiri* megaliths; the custom of constructing stone circles is long gone. After cremation, deemed as the first burial, the remains of the dead are put inside an earthen pitcher and buried in sacred ground as a second burial, over which a *sasandiri* is raised. The *birdiri* is later ritualistically erected in memory of the departed. The non-tribal villagers in Jharkhand refer to such standing memorial stones as *birkhod* or *birkhol* in Hindi.

Sat-Bharwaan

Sat-Bharwaan or *sat-marawa* is a non-tribal, Dalit ritual of bone disposal that, though once popular across the northern tract of India and Pakistan, is now only vaguely prevalent among a few Dalit communities in Jharkhand. In this particular ritual, conducted subsequent to the cremation of the dead, the bones along with the ash of the deceased are placed in an earthen pitcher and buried next to a menhir, or even immersed in a flowing river. The pot may also contain a single or a pair of small conical iron implements, connected to one other with a slender iron chain, called *singies* (Plate 37), into which the ash and bone fragments of the dead are inserted and then jammed with a circular iron lid or lids.

Although ritualistic burials are alluded to in the Upanishads, megaliths do not find a mention in the Vedic corpus. Furthermore, while references of these tombs are scant in the Buddhist Tripitaka, Tamil Sangam literature cites the megaliths of South India quite extensively.

AS TEMPLES

In ancient Europe, the entire landscape was believed to be alive and sacred, and, as discussed earlier, the ancients worshipped the earth as the Mother Goddess (Cope 1998, 11). Peter Gow (1995, 43–62) shows that, for the locals, the Bayo Urubanka river was lived as a 'human landscape'. In quite a similar manner, the landscapes of Chota Nagpur of Jharkhand, too, were held as human landscapes (Damodaran 2002, 135, 158).

Therefore, megalithic burials, by virtue of being sited in such a living landscape that was held as the Mother Goddess, and being associated to spirits, ancestors, and Goddess worship, are also deemed as temple-burials, given that these stone burials were adjudged to be shrines of the Mother Goddess since hoary times. Cope believes that megaliths were indeed the first-ever monuments of human kind (Cope 1998, 3). Cousens (1926) writes that many dolmens in South India were shrines. He further writes about hundreds of dolmens that were erected by women pilgrims between Badami and Mahakuta. These megaliths thus seem to have been sacrosanct to them. Other scholars and researchers including Meaden also maintain that megalithic settings may be regarded as shrines or temples (Meaden 1992, 27). In his yet unpublished book (shared with the author), Meaden demonstrates that the 17-stone megalithic circle at Drombeg in Ireland is indeed a finely planned temple and whose core values apply just as well to Stonehenge.

In accordance with this very ancient tradition, these temple-burials in Jharkhand are ritualistically worshipped, be it annually or intermittently, both by tribals and Dalits (although Dalits do not follow megalithic funerary practices anymore).

Evidence shows that humankind held women in the highest esteem during prehistory; several communities of this era were matriarchal and pledged allegiance to the fertility cult. The faint remnants of this cult are still apparent in many Hindu rites and customs as also those of the tribal societies of Jharkhand. Female genitals and pregnant women and their wombs, being appendages of the now obsolete fertility cults of the all-pervading Mother Goddess, were held in the highest regard and hence worshipped (Das 2009, 43–49). Megalithic structures are relics of these fecundity cults—graves were placed inside the earth as it was considered the Mother Goddess's womb (Meaden 1992, 27). The idea behind megalithic graves was to replicate the Great Goddess's womb, because of which, round the world, the dead were usually placed in the foetal position within their graves. Scholars and archaeologists like T. Cyriax believe that the ancients regarded the earth as their mother, into which the dead were buried and tombs were created in the likes of the mother (Cyriax 1921). The core belief behind placing the dead inside Mother Earth, therefore, was a return to the mother's womb (Das 2009). This idea is further discussed by Gimbutas (1991) and Meaden (1992).

The *Satapatha Brahmana* asserts that graves (this may not apply explicitly to megalithic graves though) are to be established on barren soil, on levelled ground that is inclined towards the north, with a south-easterly flowing river nearby. It further states that these monuments should not only be exposed to the sun but should also be approachable for worship. This reference from a sacred corpus confirms that graves were indeed held sacred and worshipped as shrines.

During Vedic times, too, the earth was held as the Mother and ashes were poured (after cremation) from the *kumbha* (pot) into her womb (inside the earth). The pitcher (*kumbha*), according to Kosambi, is also the Mother's womb (Kosambi 1962) and so are pots and urns. The pot to tribals was symbolic of the womb while the water inside was sacred (Van Exem 1982, 151) as it induced pregnancy. Dead bodies, particularly those of children, have been found buried inside urns with megaliths raised on them in honour of the Great Goddess. Burials inside vaults, as in *sasandiris* or in cairns or stone circles, also subscribe to the womb-burial theory of the fertility cults.

Hills, as discussed in the previous chapter, were considered sacred, believed to be the breasts and vulva of the Mother Goddess. As a result, these sacred hills were linked to megaliths by way of alignments. The significance of such alignments, however, is lost to us today. Perhaps this was done to associate sacred Mother hills to the megaliths, so that the latter may share the former's female fertility properties, elevating these monuments to fertility temples (Das 2009).

The lighting of lamps beside *birdiris* or *sasandiris* around the vernal equinox or the winter solstice, or the pouring of mustard oil on them, are but a few among several rituals of ancestor-worship prevalent among the megalithic tribes of

Jharkhand. Ancestor-worship was a component of the ancient fertility cults.

WITH ASTRONOMICAL CONNOTATIONS

That many prehistoric megaliths in Europe were constructed with astronomical alignments has been well known for centuries. Unlike in the West, the concept of astronomical megaliths is unknown in India and hence not recognised by mainstream archaeology. The study of this dormant field of Indian megaliths, though still in its formative years, is now being carried out fervently by a new breed of researchers in the country.

Mainstream Indian archaeology does not associate megaliths with astronomy. For archaeologists, megaliths are nothing but burials and/or memorials of the dead. To them, the study and investigation of the surface architecture of megaliths is unimportant as a megalith is characterised by the burial it keeps. Several stone circles or other types of megaliths that did not yield any mortuary remains are generally considered to be memorials.

Nevertheless, it was F.R. Allchin, the noted archaeologist, who, in 1956 in India, authored a pioneering paper called 'The Stone Alignments of Southern Hyderabad' (Allchin 1956, 133), giving reference to 40 megaliths including Nilurallu, Hanamsagar, Vibhuthihalli, etc. in the South Hyderabad region that did not yield any mortal remains but demonstrated astronomical alignments. Regarding Vibhutihalli, Allchin's research showed that the stones inside the megalithic complex were astronomically aligned towards the cardinal points in addition to being positioned in parallel lines and spaced at regular intervals. He also discovered two distinct types of alignments that he later categorised as square and diagonal alignments. The menhirs in a few of these astronomical megaliths were arranged in grids and aligned to the cardinal directions (Menon 2012, 17). Subsequently, Paddayya observed that the stones at the Hanamsagar site were arranged in 50 rows with each row comprising 50 stones, i.e. a total of 2,500 stones! (Paddayya 1995, 23–27).

Research carried out on the megaliths of Nilurallu, Murardoddi, and Brahmagiri in Andhra Pradesh and Karnataka by scholars of the Indian Institute of Astrophysics (Rao and Thakur 2011, 74–82) (Rao 1993, 67–77) showed that these shrines manifest astronomical links and are orientated towards equinoctial and solstitial sunrises and sunsets. Studies conducted by various scholars under the aegis of Tata Institute of Fundamental Research on the megaliths of Nilaskal and Baise in Karnataka have also revealed many astronomical alignments—a 'solstitial grid formation' and a 'framing' of solstice sunrises and sunsets, etc.—by way of the positioning of the stones in these megalithic complexes (Menon and Vahia 2011).

D.H. Gordon cites Carlleyle, who had acknowledged the noteworthy 'measurements in a druidical or magian sense' of the now demolished Deosa stone circles of Rajasthan (Gordon 1997, 183). Several prominent megaliths, such as those at Burzahom in Kashmir and Asota in Pakistan, have been found to be non-sepulchral and yielded no human remains (Ghosh 1990). The megalithic complex at Asota is yet known to the locals as a sun temple, reminding us of the prehistoric megalithic temple's astronomical links. Excavations of numerous stone circles have shown that several of these monuments are devoid of any burials (Deglurkar and Lad 1992).

Comprehensive and meticulous studies by the author and his team of a few megalithic sites in Jharkhand, such as those at Katia Murbey, Chano, Birbir, Punkri Burwadih, Furuka, etc., revealed that astronomy and geometry had been employed in their planning and construction. A few of these astronomically built stone temples demonstrate that, apart from holding the remains of the dead, these structures must also have served as observatories for the transits of the sun, moon, and the stars. Perhaps these monuments served as calendars for the prehistoric tribal communities, all possibly in keeping with their fertility rites.

Contrary to Siddhantic astronomy, developed much later by Aryan scholars with foundations in calculations of the transits and motions of the planets, the sun, and other stellar bodies, pre/non-Aryan tribal astronomy was based on observations of the transits and positions of the sun, moon, and the stars. This approach is better known as observational or horizon astronomy. Thus, megalithic astronomers positioned their observatories fortified with their understanding of such observational astronomy. The orientation of megalithic temples towards cardinal points and equinoctial and solstitial sunrises and sunsets perhaps allowed the ancients to make use of these dates to conduct the various fertility festivals and rites.

Most of these rituals disappeared with time but a few are still prevalent in both the Hindu and tribal belief systems. The hypothesis that the sun inseminates the earth while shining in its full glory during the summer solstice may have led the ancients to hold the sunrise of this day as sacred. Ambubachi, the significant three-day Earth Goddess festival in the Mother temple of Kamakhya in eastern India, still begins from a day or two subsequent to the midsummer sunrise, when the sun travels farthest in the northern hemisphere, commencing its return journey to the winter solstice the following day (Das 2014, 31).

The prevalent belief is that Mother Earth menstruates for three days beginning from around the summer solstice/Ambubachi, following which she becomes fertile. No tilling of the earth is done then; care is taken to not drop any heavy utensils on the ground lest Mother Earth be pained on these lean days of her menstruation. Several Goddess temples in Assam, Bihar, Odisha, and Bengal remain closed during this time. On the fourth day, she is believed to have regained her fertility; farming of the land hence commences with fanfare. Such agricultural fertility festivals must have their origins in the fertility cults of antiquity. Based on his studies, Meaden, too, maintained that fertility rituals were practised by farming communities (Meaden 1992, 18).

Orientation of the megalithic complexes of Bayen and Singhani and of a few stones at the Chano, Katia Murbey, and Punkri Burwadih megalithic temples towards the midsummer sunrise was perhaps done to mark the day that augmented the fertility of both the tribes' womenfolk and their farming lands. Such orientation of megalithic burials towards the summer solstice sunrise may also have been done for the interred to receive blessings from the fertility goddesses.

Several menhirs in and around Hazaribagh have been found to be aligned towards the winter solstice sunrise. The reason behind this cannot be firmly ascertained. Nonetheless, my deliberations point to the *'jang-topa'*-type bone-burying tribal rituals (Sinha 1997, 10), also referred to as *jang-gadiya*, that were once held on or around the winter solstice sunrise. After burying the bones of the dead on the aforementioned day, a menhir facing the midwinter sunrise was planted at the spot where the cinerary pot was buried.

Alignments also find mention in the Sanskrit text *Surya Siddhanta,* which reveals that ancient Indian cities were also connected by way of alignments. The book affirms that the *merus* or poles are connected by the *madhyarekha* or the axis of the Earth, which passes through Kurukshetra and the cities of Rohtak and Ujjain (Chakravarty 2001, 10).

MATHEMATICAL MEASUREMENTS

Examining the menhirs at various megalithic sites revealed their heights to be 18, 36, 52, 56, 66, 72, or 80 inches, and so on, which confirmed that the portion of a menhir discernible above the ground was to be of a predetermined height, demonstrating in the process that the ancients of Jharkhand indeed used a standard unit of measurement. The tools of measurement, however, may have been fingers, hands, and arms, though measuring rulers of ivory dating to 2200 BC have been unearthed from the Indus city of Lothal. Known as the Mohenjo-Daro ruler, these are divided into units of 1.32 inches (33.5 mm) and marked out in decimal subdivisions to within a claimed 0.005th of an inch. Bricks found throughout the region have dimensions that match these units (Whitelaw 2007).

Brahmanical texts such as the *Satapatha Brahmana, Apastamba Dharmasutra,* and Panini's *Astadhyayi*, too, are believed to contain various units of measurement. It is, however, Chanakya who is assumed to have authored the eminent *Arthashastra*, documenting the units of measurement prevalent during the Mauryan period, which are as under:

- 1 *angula* (finger) (tentative breadth of a finger): equivalent to ¾th of an inch
- 4 *angulas*: 3"
- 8 *angulas*: 1 *dhanurmushti* (fist with raised thumb); 6"
- 12 *angulas*: 1 *vitasta* or *vitta* or *artani* (distance between the thumb and the little finger while stretching out the palm); 9"
- 2 *vittas*: 1 *hatha* or *hasta* or 1 arm from the elbow to the tip of the middle finger; 18"
- 4 *hathas* or *hastas* or *artanis*: 1 *danda*; 72"

And so on. The practice of using the arm and the thumb as units of measurement is still popular among rural artisans.

Interestingly, across the state of Jharkhand, there is a preponderance of the term *bawan* meaning 52, such that the name of a hill in Hazaribagh is Bawanwey or 'the 52nd one', to which several megaliths are aligned.

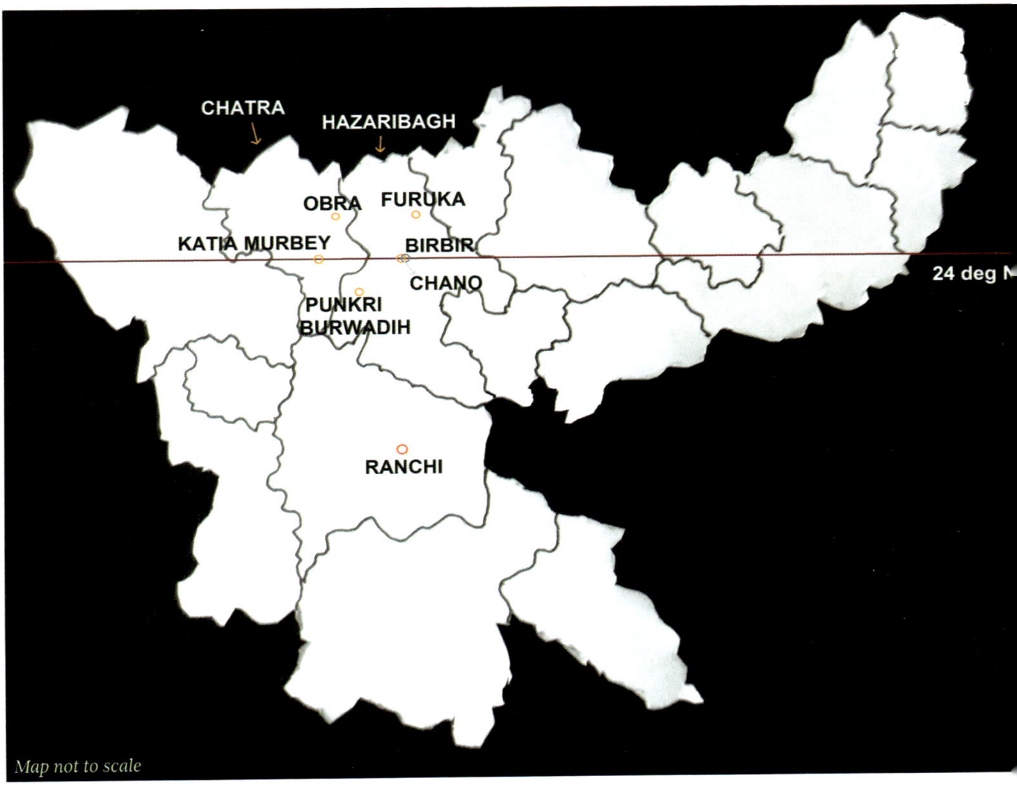
CHATRA
HAZARIBAGH
OBRA
FURUKA
KATIA MURBEY
BIRBIR
CHANO
24 deg N
PUNKRI
BURWADIH
RANCHI
Map not to scale

THE SITES

As discussed earlier, the ancients established megalithic sites in landscapes encircled by hills—most definitely an arduous and demanding task. When Antony Roper Crerar, the celebrated archaeoastronomer from Wales, visited Chano, he was so impressed with the author's discovery of the site that he later wrote to him: 'They [the megalithic astronomers] undoubtedly recognised the significance of your latitude for allowing hex-sectioning of the circle ... and possibly, if they came from elsewhere, had predicted this situation and calculated where to find it by long experience from establishment of other alignments in territories to the north or south of you.' He further added, 'the trained astronomer would immediately recognise the potential of the Chano plain ringed by mountains when walking into it on a clear day and indeed, might have been actively searching for it.'

Ancient megalithic astronomers hex-sectioned the circular horizon (forming a cross-within-a-circle) by aligning the megalithic temples to hills. Such alignments at a given site can delight any onlooker with the aptitude to appreciate the magnificence of this ancient science of orientation.

The following pages take a closer look at the design and layout of each temple as also their unique characteristics. Every megalithic temple is established with meticulous planning and manifests intricate design principles—a perception that has hitherto eluded us. How the astronomer-priests envisaged the desired layout of stones within a complex as also the positioning of the entire complex on the ground prior to installation remains unknown to us.

To explore the mysteries of these enigmatic astronomical megalithic temples, the author had to undertake countless visits to such sites, focusing on the bits that may have evaded him on his previous visits. Today, equipped with an insight into the secrets of these archaeoastronomical megalithic temples, he firmly believes that such stone shrines are indeed timeless creations of humankind and should be considered in league with the other significant monuments of the land.

Until now, such astronomical temples have only been found in the Hazaribagh and Chatra districts of Jharkhand; more such megalithic temples must exist elsewhere in the state, waiting to be discovered. In case no other such temple is found in any of the other districts, then the reason behind the same could form the basis of a follow-up study.

CHANO

Latitude: 23°59'24" N | Longitude: 85°25'52.1" E

Accessibility

Chano is located six kilometres east of Hazaribagh town. Drive on the Bagodar highway to arrive at the bend to Saraoni, proceeding another 300 metres along it. The megaliths lie hidden in a field adjacent to the boundary of a house, about 100 metres to the right of the road.

The megalithic site of Chano is an ancient tribal *hargarhi* comprising five arbitrarily arranged *sasandiri* stones. The

Plate 5

complex's diminutive spread makes it appear insignificant to anyone who is oblivious to the contents of this remarkable site.

For better understanding the megalithic temple at hand, let us label the stones at the site in the following order:

- Two triangles of comparable sizes: **A** and **B**
- The phallus: **C**
- The East–West recumbent stone: **D**
- The largest pointer stone: **E**
- The mid-point of the gap between **A** and **B**: **F**
- An imaginary spot to the north of the phallus on the North–South axis: **G** (Drawing 1) (Plates 6, 7, 8, and 9)

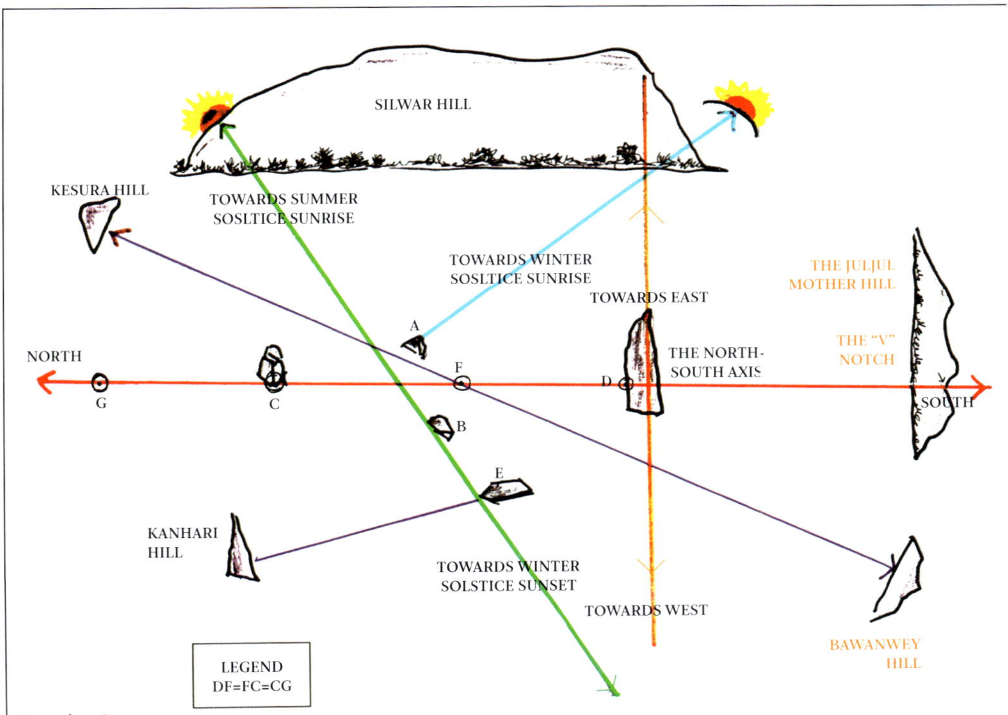

Drawing 1

Description

D is a trim reclining stone. The stone is carved to a length of 1.83 metres (the standard 72 inches) and placed in an East–West orientation (Plate 9). Small circular indentations known as cupules can be seen engraved on it in an East–West bearing. Cupules were, in many situations, meant to be female symbols (Meaden 1999, 5). The question thus arises whether the stone D featuring cupules and the specific lengthwise dimension of 72 inches for an ancient menhir (erect or reclining) is symbolic of a female stone. The idea of male and female stones was once quite common in Madagascar (Cope 1998, 195). The Kachha Nagas believe dolmens to be female stones, while for the Angami Nagas, the erect and the recumbent stone represent the male and the female principles respectively (Hutton 1922, 58, 60). The Khasis in Meghalaya accord female principles to reclining stones as they are laid in honour of *Ka-Yobai*, the primordial, all-powerful Mother Goddess (Chakravorty 1993, 24).

The highlight of Chano is a 74cm-tall phallus with the glans labelled as **C** (Plates 6 and 7). The organ is fabulously crafted and invokes awe at the ancient sculptor's sense of aesthetics and superb rendition. Chano, in contrast to the other megalithic sites of Jharkhand, does not feature the commonly seen 'tall' menhirs. A wonderfully hewn and polished stone with a pointed

---

DRAWING 1 *Layout of the Chano megalithic site. Sketch showing the alignments towards the hills, and the sunrises and sets of the solstices.*

PLATE 5 *The astronomical megalithic temple of Chano. Credit: Ms Bubu Das*

Plate 6

C
F
B
A

Plate 7

Plate 8

top, marked **E** and with a length of 1.68 m (the standard 66 inches), stands inclined at about 52 degrees and is the tallest menhir at the site (Plates 5 and 8).

Two stone triangles of varying sizes, labelled **A** and **B**, with peaks that point in opposite directions (Plates 5 and 11), are also found in the temple. Stone triangles are a common element in a few of the many megalithic sites in Hazaribagh—a feature not encountered elsewhere (Das 2008, 181–185). Round the world, triangles with their apexes pointing to the sky are held to be phallic representations, and the inverse is deemed symbolic of the female vulva. These symbols are also encountered in tantric rituals. It is difficult to ascertain the significance of such triangles at megalithic sites; these perhaps suggest the prevalence of tantra-type rites among the megalith-makers of the region, a precursor to Tantric Buddhism. However, the triangles at Chano appear to have also been used as pointers apart from serving as phallic representations.

Alignments, Astronomy, and Geometry

As discussed earlier, the presence of hills on the horizon was a prerequisite for establishing megaliths. As such, the temple at Chano, too, is aligned to the hills that circumscribe it. The placement and orientation of both the megalithic site and

---

PLATE 6 *The Chano megaliths*

PLATE 7 *The phallus*

PLATE 8 *The large pointer stone* E *with an arrowed tip points towards Kanheri hill in the distance.*

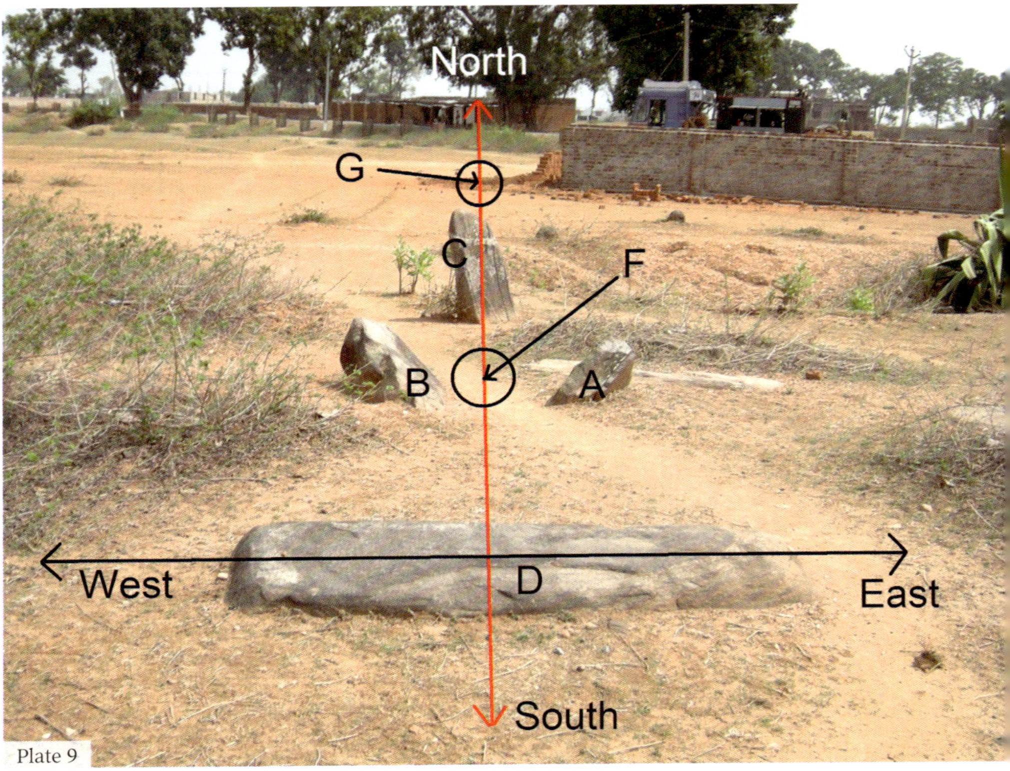

Plate 9

Plate 10

a number of its stones reveal the ancient megalith-makers' knowledge of geometry, proportions, and astronomy.

Standing in the middle of the shrine, one can observe that the temple is located precisely 'on' the unseen line connecting Bawanwey and Kesura hills, located at 220° SSW and 40° NNE respectively (Drawing 1). The stone **E**, placed at an angle of 52°, points towards Kanheri hill on the horizon, located at about 320° NNW (Plates 5, 6, and 8). Standing adjacent to **E**, one realises that the stone along with the phallus **C** form a straight line with the conical Kesura hill on the NE horizon (Plate 10). The site is also oriented towards Silwar hill, situated a few hundred metres due east. The cup-marked recumbent female stone **D**, placed in an East–West orientation and assumed to be the cover of a grave, has its slender end pointing to the east towards a cluster of stones atop the right flank of Silwar hill (Plate 9).

The smallest stone in the complex, triangle **A** has been placed in such a manner that it points precisely towards an unnamed hill from behind which the sun is seen rising on the mornings of the winter solstice, i.e. 22/23 December (Plate 12). Unfortunately, as seen in the plate, a house has cropped up between the hill and the megalithic site, obstructing any alignments between the two. The triangular pointer **B** along with **E** is aligned

---

PLATE 9 *The photograph explains all. Photo taken standing on the North–South axis facing north.*

PLATE 10 *The largest pointer* E *and the phallus* C *are perfectly aligned to Kesura hill in the horizon.*

Plate 11

to the winter solstice sunset of 22/23 December (Plate 13) (Drawing 1). Standing opposite to pointer stone **E** and in alignment to it and **B**, one observes that the stones are positioned in a perfect straight line with the rising sun on the summer solstice mornings of 20/21 June, seen from the rear of the left slope of Silwar hill (Drawing 1).

In the process of our examination of the site, we discovered that the site's North–South axis had been created by a very intelligent arrangement of the stones. The axis, touching the phallus **C**, extends through the space between the two triangles, simultaneously intersecting the East–West recumbent stone **D**, and eventually crosses through the 'V' feature on the right flank of Juljul hill, due south of the megaliths (Plate 11).

The 'V' shape is widely considered to be symbolic of the female vulva and representative of the Mother Goddess. Crouching at a certain spot on this North–South axis of the temple and gazing to the south towards Juljul hill, one observes that the phallus 'fits' on to the 'V' shape of the same hill, in essence canonising sexual intercourse—a major accessory of the fertility cult (this 'engineering' is also duplicated at the Birbir megalithic site—refer to plate 48). From this point, we were indeed astonished to catch sight of another dramatic image, that of **A** and **B**, the away-facing triangles, 'framing' the recumbent 'female' stone **D**

PLATE 11 *Photograph taken facing due south while standing on the North–South axis, which finally passes through the 'V' notch on Juljul hill. The photograph also illustrates the arrangement of the framing of stone D by the two pointers A and B on the same axis. Credit: Prantik Das*

Plate 12

Plate 13

from the sides as the phallus gracefully 'lifts' **D** from the middle (Plate 11). We marked the spot from where we witnessed this remarkable sight as **G**. We also discovered that shifting even a little from **G** ruined this observational set-up. One, however, needs to take into account that it is on this female stone **D** that the North–South and East–West axes intersect.

The intangible model at hand, created by a precise positioning of stones, appears to be a symbolic union of the male phallus and the female recumbent stone—components of the now obsolete fecundity cult. Meaden believes that the altered positioning of stones with respect to the landscape in a megalithic complex was effected to depict the sacred union of the Sky God and Mother Earth (Meaden 1992, 53).

Dimensions

Looking at the alignments of the Chano temple complex, one can appreciate that the prehistoric megalith-makers adhered to meticulous planning for the creation of the shrine, not only for burial purposes or for observing the movements of the sun, but also to generate this amazing visual by way of sagacious alignments.

The creation of such a dramatic image, employing a witty arrangement of the stones, reveals the brilliance of ancient

---

PLATE 12 *The smallest triangle A points precisely towards the winter solstice sunrise. The newly constructed building obstructs the view of the sunrise from behind a hill in the horizon.*

PLATE 13 *The two stones E and B are positioned in straight line with the winter solstice sunset.*

megalithic engineering. But to understand how the ancient engineers were able to create this observational set-up, viewed precisely from the spot **G**, one needs to measure the distances between the stones. In the process of surveying, we observed that the distances between **G** and **C**, **C** and **F**, and **F** and **D** were similar (Drawing 1) (Plate 9). Thus, the model of the sacred union as viewed from **G** is a result of placing the stones at equal distances, achieved deliberately to produce the image (Drawing 1) (Plates 9 and 11).

Archaeological Appraisal

Within a radius of three kilometres of Chano exists a large ancient cupule site—an archaeological site comprising large rocks featuring numerous cupules—as also several prehistoric megaliths of varying architectural styles. About 300 metres to the west of the site, a dried river channel reveals that the banks of the once-flowing river may have sustained human habitation. Pieces of iron slag lay scattered in the fields around the megaliths, confirming iron smelting in the past by tribes such as the Asur, Agaria, Karmali, Lohra, etc.

Shards of black, red, painted red, black and red, and black-on-red pottery have been collected from round the complex and from a pit wall adjacent to it (Plate 14). A small artefact that could be a portion of a bone flute (Plate 15), a celt, a blade, and a point were also extracted from the same trench. Many

---

PLATE 14 *Various potteries include black, inscribed, polished red, black-and-red collected from a pit near the Chano megalithic site.*

iron implements such as a nail cutter, an arrowhead, an iron tattoo needle, and even a dual-serpent-head brass bangle have been extracted by the plough (Plate 16). Excavation of the site is essential to discern the type of burial inside the *hargarhi*, learn about the builders of this amazing megalithic complex, study the grave yields, and to accurately date the site.

Many megaliths across the world as also that of Chano have been found to be aligned towards the summer solstice sunrise of 20/21 June. We have already discussed the reasons for considering the midsummer sunrise as sacred, which was indeed a very significant fertility festival for them. Therefore,

Plate 14

Plate 15

Plate 16

observing the sunrises and sunsets on these days with the help of the directional stones perhaps allowed the astronomer-priests to identify these dates and initiate the fertility ceremonies. Thus we may conclude that Chano, like many other astronomical megaliths, apart from being a burial site, was also an observatory of the sun for the ancient megalith-using communities, to function as their calendar. However, Chano does not feature pointer stones to facilitate viewing the equinox sunrise.

The visual model of the Sacred or Divine Union created by the geometrical positioning of the stones was perhaps realised for a fertility ritual that is unknown to us. For that reason, a burial in such a significant monument, one that is connected both to the sacred hills and to the sun, may have been thought to assist in the deceased's next life; a belief in regeneration or reincarnation was very much a part of the fertility cults.

Chano was once also a temple of the non-tribal cattle herders, who staunchly believed that their *detas* (gods) resided in the burials, beneath the stones.

PLATE 15 *A broken fragment of a bone relic, possibly that of a flute, extracted from a pit next to a megalith.*

PLATE 16 *Iron implements such as a tattoo needle, a nail cutter, and a brass bangle unearthed by ploughing around the megalithic temple.*

FURUKA

Latitude: 24°4'40.80" N | Longitude: 85°29'51.36" E

Accessibility

Drive till the Ichak More on national highway (NH) 33, located about 13 kilometres north of Hazaribagh, and turn right towards Punai. Driving past the villages of Ichak and Kariatpur, one can reach the solitary menhir in a field just before the village Furuka.

Description

This solitary menhir, resembling a pillar, stands in the middle of nowhere, and yet, when in the company of this remarkable stone, one is not quite alone. One is mystified, wondering the reason why the stone was placed here. Perhaps it was meant to mark the boundary of some village—a village that may have existed here in the past. Could it be the memorial of an eminent person who passed away very long ago? Or did it serve an astronomical purpose for some villages in remote antiquity?

Architecture and Alignments

An examination of the three sharp vertical edges and other characteristics of the stone reveals the use of precise mathematics and astronomy. The accurate positioning of the

---

DRAWING 2 *The layout of Furuka showing its alignments towards the cardinal points and the menhir is positioned exactly at the intersection of these alignments.*

menhir manifests a precise cross in the circular horizon as the menhir stands at the intersection of alignments with the hills towards the cardinal points (Drawing 2).

One of the three edges of the megalith is oriented towards Bawanwey hill to the south while its converse edge very accurately points to a peak of the Telaiya range to the north. The third perpendicular edge indicates true east (Plate 17). Whether or not there exists a hill due east is not discernible as the horizon is obscured by dense foliage. The crown of the stone is remarkable as it bears what appears to be the sector of a circle, with a gradual slope towards east (Plates 17 and 18).

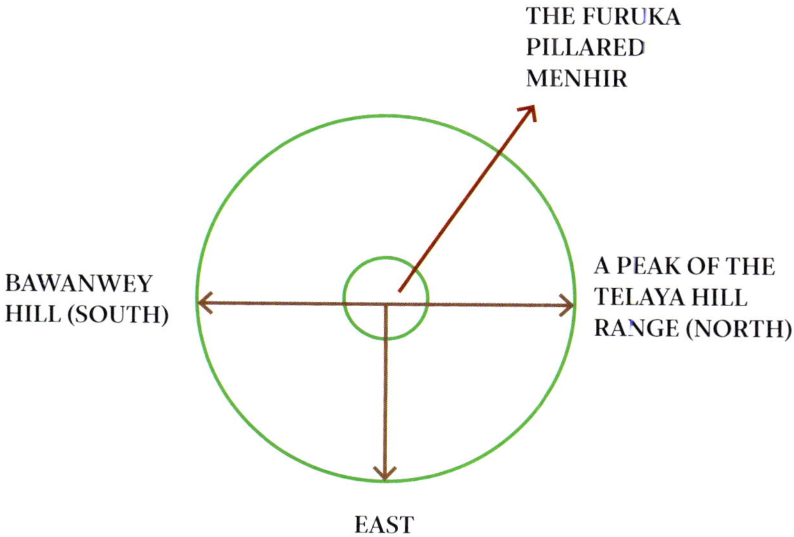

Drawing 2

Plate 17

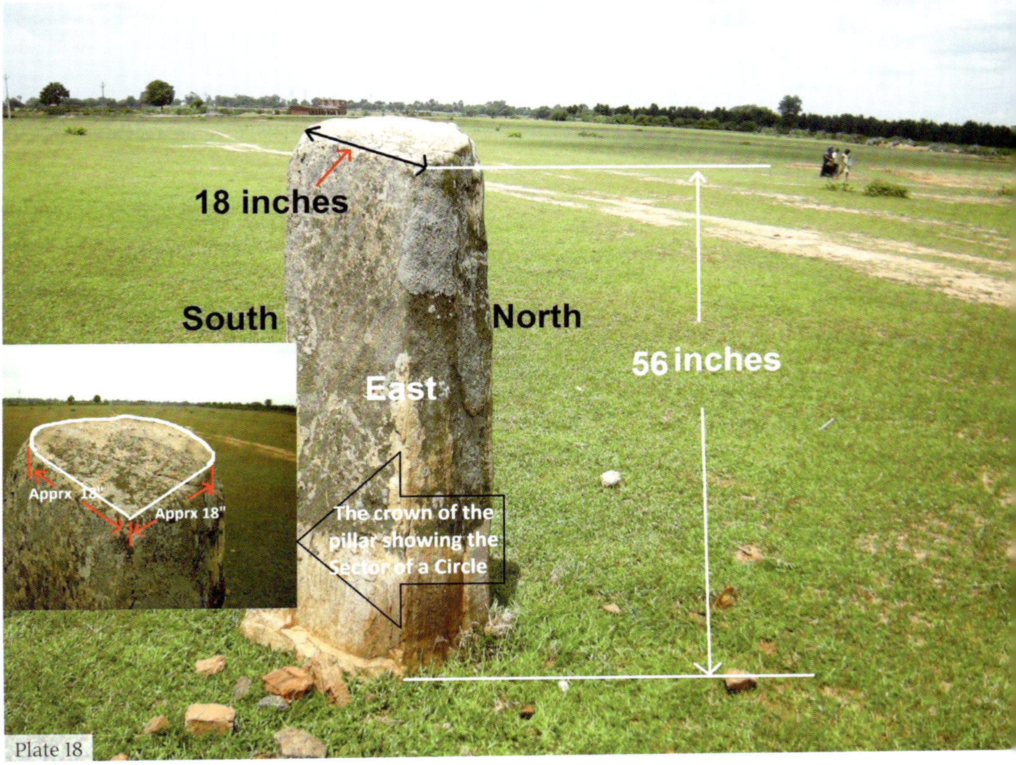

Plate 18

The find of iron slags around this ancient megalith suggests the presence of iron-smelting tribes in the area in the past.

Dimensions and Mathematics

The dimensions of this megalithic column reveal a prevalence of the standard measurements among megaliths in the past. Both the northern and southern perpendiculars stand approximately 1.524 metres or about 60 inches tall. The height of the eastern vertical edge and the length of the so-called 'radius' of the assumed sector of the circle on top are 1.422 and 0.457 metres respectively. If converted to inches, one finds that these were prepared in accordance to the standard megalithic measurements of 56 and 18 inches respectively.

The purpose behind the creation of this mathematical and astronomical model remains unknown to us.

PLATE 17 *The hewing of this pillared menhir reveals stunning astronomy. The left and right edges point due north and south respectively, whereas the front vertical edge is aligned towards the equinoctial sunrise due east. Observe the crown of the pillar; it has been sculpted as a sector of a circle.*

PLATE 18 *Photograph reveals that the standard megalithic measurements have been used in the Furuka pillar.*

PUNKRI BURWADIH

Latitude: 23°87'20" N | Longitude: 85°14'5" E

Accessibility

Drive about 22 km to the south-west of Hazaribagh towards Barkagaon village. It indeed is quite a delightful drive via a hilly road with sal (*Shorea robusta*) trees flanking either side. One gradually descends to level roads, crossing the winding and picturesque Lohsighna and Likhlahi Ghats. The megalithic temple of Punkri Burwadih is easily discernible, being located on elevated ground, to the left of the highway to Barkagaon.

Site

The author's first visit to the complex some 20 years ago had him seriously contemplating that Punkri Burwadih was not an ordinary megalithic burial site; there had to be something more to it than met the eye. Conversing with the old-timers of the village, he learnt that Punkri and Burwadih were once separate villages that were later merged, assuming then its present name.

Barely a few hundred metres to the south-west of the site was once a village called Gordaha. The name Gordaha is definitely indicative of the megaliths, formed by the combination of the

---

PLATE 19 *The astronomical observatory of Punkri Burwadih.*

Plate 19

words *gor* and *daha*, the former meaning a burial or the act of burying the dead, and the latter denoting cremation.

The megalithic temple can be seen located on a gradually elevated stretch of land. The site is encircled by the uninterrupted hill ranges of Amjhori, Bhelwahi, Tandwa, and Mahudi. However, a single opening is visible to the south-east of the site.

Architecture

A stone circle stands on the southern side of the temple complex. Planted in the middle of this circle is a stone phallus with a height of 0.7112 metres (28 inches) (Plate 20). The circle consists of five recumbent stones as also a tall menhir marked **B**, about 1.5 metres (58 inches) in height. The circle may comprise the

Plate 20

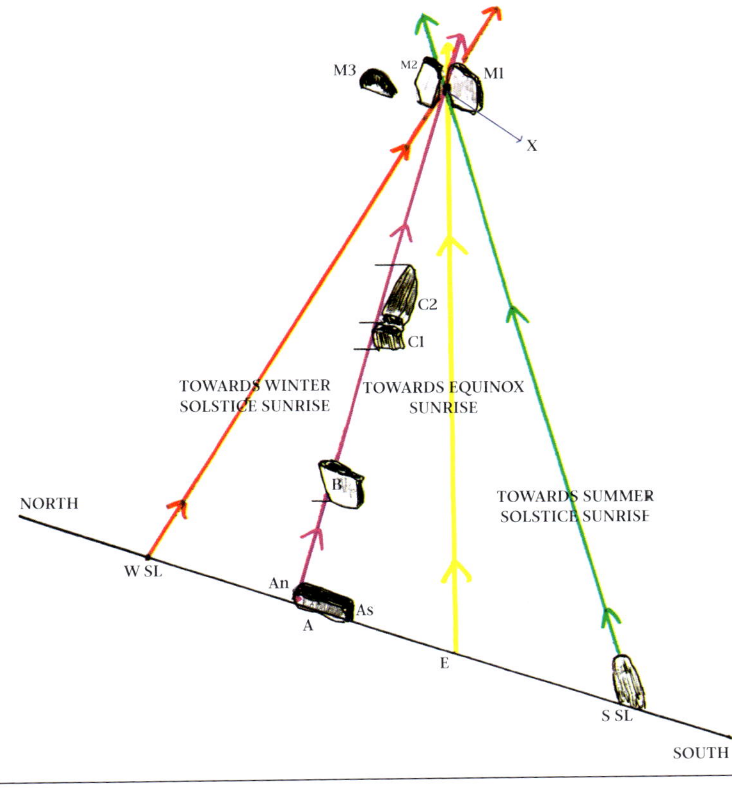

Drawing 3

burial while the menhir **B** probably marks the direction of the head of the corpse. However, this is just conjecture; the truth will only be revealed subsequent to an excavation.

Such stones are regarded as soul stones. The popular myth associated with such stones is that in the mornings, the soul of the deceased, assuming the shape of a bird, perches on top of the menhir and thereafter flies to the nearby farming fields to hunt for food, returning at day end to re-enter the burial after relaxing for a while on the menhir (Commissioner, Department of Archaeology and Museums, Government of Andhra Pradesh 2001, 46, 47). The stone circle conspicuously displays the sacred cross-within-a-circle by way of alignments of the stones with each other and with the hills in the landscape.

From every direction, the temple reveals an outstanding relationship with the encircling hills, apparent from the alignments of the stones towards them. The stones of the monument are aligned towards one another, towards the cardinal points, and also towards the prominent bulges, crevices, and peaks of the encompassing hills.

The small stone **A** (Drawing 3), with an approximate length and height of 1.016 metres (40 inches) and 0.254 metres (10 inches)

PLATE 20 *The circle formed by the megalithic temple may comprise the burial. At the middle of the circle stands the phallic stone.*

DRAWING 3 *The layout of Punkri Burwadih. Observe how splendidly the stones were arranged by the ancient megalithic engineers.*

respectively, perches behind the earlier described menhir **B** in a North–South orientation and is the meridian stone of the temple. The left edge of stone **A**, pointing due north, is labelled **An**, with the right flank, indicating south, marked **As**. A trapezoidal emboss can be seen in the centre of the surface of **A** that faces the menhir **B**. Attentive observation reveals that the left edge **An** of the stone **A** is aligned to a conspicuous bulge of Amjhori hill, located to its north (Plate 21), while the right rim **As** is aligned to the left edge of Mahudi hill to the south.

M1 and **M2** are a pair of adjacent menhirs that are cut and positioned in such a manner that a 'V' shape is produced. The midpoint in the space between the two menhirs is marked **X**. In between the menhir **B** and the point **X** lies another menhir that

Plate 21

is broken in two. The smaller remnant of this menhir, marked **C1** and found buried in the ground, loosely resembles stone **A**, while the larger broken piece of the recumbent menhir is held as **C2**. **An** and the left edge of **C1** form a perfect straight line with **X** (Drawing 3).

Several stones feature cupules and engraved designs like that of a game board on them, of which the latter could have been made by the villagers. However, a small engraved recumbent human figure on **M2** is interesting.

Various Alignments

Cradling—Walking about 100 metres to the west of the temple, one can view one of the most spectacular alignments—the entire temple complex can be seen brilliantly positioned between the two, breast-shaped Bhelwahi hills (Plate 22). The view, however, is best seen lying prostrate on the field and looking ahead. One is even more astonished to find that this arrangement is actually 'on' the East–West axis.

This display was perhaps designed by the custodians of the temple to inspire awe in the rustic minds of the prehistoric pilgrim.

Framing—The temple captures the changing forms of the encompassing hill range from various spots. Such forms of the

---

PLATE 21 *The small meridian stone A is placed in a North–South orientation. The photograph shows how impeccably A is aligned to the hump of Amjhori hill to the north.*

Plate 22

Plate 23

hills were held sacred in the ancient world. If one walks up to the solitary recumbent stone on the south of south-west periphery of the temple and then turns to look at the megaliths, one can witness the image of the recumbent Mother Goddess. What one sees is a naturally undulating shape in the Amjhori mountain range resembling a reclined pregnant woman—a form that was believed to be of the ubiquitous recumbent Mother Goddess during prehistoric times.

This form is made conspicuous by an intelligent positioning of the menhirs **M1** and **B**, which frame it (Plate 23). This display must have been used as a spectacle by the ancient custodians of the temple to dazzle the bucolic pilgrims. During the age of the fertility cult, hills and their parts resembling breasts or recumbent pregnant women were highly revered as Goddesses (Das 2009, 43) (Cope 1998, 66). These consecrated shapes lay hidden in the undulating hills and only the discerning eyes of the guardian priests of such temples were able to distinguish them. They would subsequently extract and showcase this sight to the pilgrims by means of framing and other alignments (Das 2009, 192).

Mirroring or Reflection—Mirroring alignments at Punkri Burwadih as also a few other megalithic temples in and

PLATE 22 *The cradling. The entire megalithic site is cradled between the breast-shaped Bhelwahi hills.*

PLATE 23 *From the viewing point indicated by the recumbent menhir, one can observe that the two menhirs here frame the recumbent pregnant form of the Amjhori mountain range.*

Plate 24

around Hazaribagh illustrate not only the megalith-makers' perception of the relationship between megaliths and the landscape, but also their knowledge of megalithic engineering by way of alignments in positioning the stones in conformity with the hills on the horizon. In order to comprehend why the three menhirs **M1**, **M2**, and **B** are where they are today, one needs to walk about 60 metres to the south-east from the centre of the megaliths.

Squatting on the ground and fixing one's gaze on the temple from this spot reveals a spellbinding sight. The menhirs **M1**, **M2**, and **B** flawlessly 'mirror' or 'reflect' the three peaks of Jugra hill range in the horizon (Plate 25). Positioning the three menhirs in relation to the three peaks of Jugra range gave rise

to a scene where the stones indeed appear to be 'mirroring' or 'reflecting' the ridges of the said range. This is a display of a simple feature, and yet it is a magnificent feat of prehistoric megalithic engineering.

Astronomy

M1, **M2**, **M3,** and **B**, like several other menhirs in Jharkhand, are oriented to the winter solstice sunrise and the summer solstice

---

PLATE 24 *Another variety of alignment. Note how the phallic stone* P *in the foreground and* M3 *are positioned in a perfect straight line with the blue slice of an unknown hill in the backdrop, which is cradled by the Bhelwahi hill range.*

PLATE 25 *Mirroring or reflection. The three menhirs M1, M2, and B are positioned in such a manner that they immaculately 'mirror' the three peaks of the Jugra hill range on the horizon.*

sunset respectively. Standing on the North–South axis at a point approximately 3.93 metres (155 inches) north of **An,** marked **Wsl** (Drawing 3), the sun can be seen rising through the V notch on winter solstice mornings.

A rope needs to be placed horizontally between **Wsl** and **Ssl**. **Ssl** is the reclining stone placed some way to the right of **As** (Drawing 3), standing at the foot of which one could view the summer solstice sunrise through the V. Today, however, a large tree blocks the view of the notch in the hill, completely obscuring the summer solstice sunrise. Shifting the viewing position along the rope in accordance to sunrises from one solstice to the other, the solar orb can be seen ascending through the V notch every morning from behind the curvilinear Amjhori hill.

On 15 February and 26/27 October, as also on 26/27 February and 15/16 October, the sunrises can be viewed through the V notch between **M1** and **M2** when standing beside **An** and **As** respectively (Plate 26). On the unseen North–South axis indicated by the rope is the designated point **E**, from where the V notch is due east. **E** is 2.36 metres to the right of **As**, standing on which the solar orb can be seen ascending through the V from behind the shapely hills on equinox mornings (Plate 27).

PLATE 26 *The alluring sunrise of 15th February and 26th October Note how accurately stone A has been positioned so that its left edge An is in perfect alignment with the sunrises of these mornings from between the menhirs M1 and M2. To its right is As that is oriented to the sunrises of 26/27 February and 15/16 October from between the same menhirs.*

PLATE 27 *The iconic photograph of the equinox sunrise from between the two menhirs M1 and M2.*

Plate 26

Plate 27

Plate 28

Moving south along the rope, one reaches the stone **Ssl** that is oriented towards the V.

To the south-west of the temple lies a pond, in which pilgrims were required to take a dip prior to performing rituals in the temple. The ancient peasant bone-burying ritual known as Sat-Bharwaan, too, was practised around megaliths till even a few decades ago. A dip in the pond was mandatory subsequent to the bone-burial ceremony.

During discussions with N. Kameswara Rao, a noted archaeoastronomer and former professor at the Indian Institute of Astrophysics, Bengaluru, the author was informed that Punkri Burwadih was located in close proximity to the tropic of Cancer.

The tropic of Cancer shifts at the slow pace of approximately 46.8 arc seconds per century. The latitude of tropic of Cancer today is 23°26'16" N while Punkri Burwadih's coordinates are 23°52'20" N. Keeping in mind the drift of the tropic of Cancer, Rao calculated that it could have passed over the Punkri Burwadih megaliths around 1518 BC! Antony Crerar, during his visit to Punkri Burwadih, too, took note of this phenomenon. He worked on this concept of the shift of the tropic of Cancer to discover that it may have crossed the megaliths round about 1550 BC.

The variation in the calculated shift of the tropic of Cancer by the two scholars is merely 32 years, but it is possible that the temple was constructed more or less around these dates, when the tropic had passed over this particular location!

The megalithic folk could not have known about the tropic of Cancer. Then why was this day of such significance to them? The answer may lie in the fact that at noon on summer solstice days, during the time when the tropic of Cancer passed over this land, there would have been no shadows of vertical objects. The astronomer-priests, perhaps for this reason, had deemed the land sacred, while summer solstice was a noteworthy day since long for the ancient people.

PLATE 28 *Curious crowds gather from all over the country to witness the rare spectacle of the sunrise through the menhirs of the Punkri Burwadih megaliths on the equinox mornings making her the only megalithic site in India to view such sunrises.*

The approximate date of 1500 BC also perfectly matches my proposed timeline of the arrival of Proto-Australoid Kolarian tribes in the region, who were perhaps the architects of the megalithic temple of Punkri Burwadih.

Dimensions

Surveying the site reveals that the stones in the temple were positioned not only with astronomical alignments but also according to simple geometry.

The menhirs **M1** and **M2** are about 1.47 metres (58 inches) and 1.65 metres (65 inches) tall respectively, and stand at a distance of 0.356 metres (14 inches) from each other. A smaller stone marked **M3,** featuring a semi-circular crown, is located in the same row at a distance of 0.711 metres (28 inches) from **M2**. This, therefore, reveals that the distance between **M2** and **M3** is actually double the gap between **M1** and **M2**.

If we join the trapezoid feature at the centre of **A** with the left edges of **B** and **C1** and extend the line to **X** (midpoint in the space between **M1** and **M2**), we find that they are in a perfect straight line.

Other hidden specifics were uncovered when further surveys were carried out—we found that the span **An–B** is the same as **As–E,** both of which are 2.36 metres (93 inches). In other words, the length **An–B** actually demonstrates the equinox viewing distance **As–E**. Measuring the space between **B** and **C1**, we found it to be equivalent to the distance between **An** and **Wsl**—approximately

3.93 metres (155 inches). As such, the distance **B–C1** apparently manifests the winter solstice viewing length of **An–Wsl**.

Encouraged by these finds of stunning similarities in the spacing of the stones, we measured the distance **E–SSL** as also **C2–X**. Astonishingly, both lengths were found to be approximately equal, i.e. 6.73 metres (265 inches or 22 feet approx.). Simply put, the span between **C2** and **X** manifests the distance between the equinox and summer solstice viewing points **E** and **SSL**.

Acoustics

During the course of a shoot, I stumbled upon a spot near the menhir **B** from where my voice resonated in open air. I promptly located the precise spot from where the reverberation was effected and noticed a small stone there peeping out from the ground. The stone, I presumed, must serve as a marker, planted by the prehistoric custodians of the temple to indicate where one needed to stand, while facing the menhir **B**, to obtain the reverberations. The indicator stone was found placed at a distance of about 1.83 metres (74 inches; near about the standard 72 inches) to the south-east of **B**.

In order to understand the engineering behind the observed resonance at this megalithic temple, I requested the assistance of the physics department at Vinoba Bhave University. Dr Navin Chandra, a professor of physics, along with other professors and postgraduate students of his department, travelled with me to Punkri Burwadih to investigate the acoustics of the site (Plate 29).

Plate 29

Their research showed that the menhir **B**, facing **M1** and **M2**, features a 70mm (28-inch) tall natural elongated parabolic depression that was facilitating the reverberations (Plate 30). They also discovered that the menhir was deliberately positioned with a slight tilt, which further enabled the resonance (Plate 31).

PLATE 29 *Photograph shows experiments on the reverberation being conducted by the professors and PG students of the Physics dept of Vinoba Bhave University. Credit: Prantik Das.*

PLATE 30 *Note the natural parabolic depression on the surface of the menhir B (marked with a yellow ellipse) and the tilt. Both these features enable the echo to occur.*

Throughout the world, echoes and reverberations are found to be an integral part of numerous ancient monuments and megaliths. It seems the builders of Punkri Burwadih, too, desired such acoustics in their temple, granting significance to the edifice. Therefore, to achieve this, the ancients must have searched for a stone with a natural depression that could generate the reverberations for some specific ritual. When found, the desired portion of the stone was probably cut out of the parent stone in its present form and buried at an angle so that a resonance could be obtained at the required

Plate 30

distance from **B**. The entire act was a great accomplishment in prehistoric engineering.

I further noted that the most impressive effect was obtained not by squatting on the ground but by standing a little to the right of the marker stone and speaking loudly while bowing the head (Plate 32).

Plate 31

The resonance of menhir **B** was probably very cunningly used by the astronomer-priests to trick innocent and rustic peasants. The menhir is perhaps the memorial/burial stone of a priest/*pahan* of the shrine, who may have been a powerful oracle performing magic, healing people, etc. The menhir may have been held as the petrified form of the dead priest; hence, the sacred stone that emits echoes was probably feared as the 'oracle stone'. Even after his or her death, people may have continued consulting the priest by standing at the marker stone and speaking to the

PLATE 31 *Profile of the menhir B demonstrates the incline that assists in the reverberation. Prantik looks on as Abhisek and I work on the measurements of the oracular stone B. Credit: Krishna Sahu*

PLATE 32 *The group stands at the marker stone and address the stone B for the reverberation.*

menhir **B**, regarded then as the oracle stone, for a fee to the custodian priest for salvation from their afflictions.

Function

Punkri Burwadih was indeed built to serve as an observatory for monitoring the passage of the sun and perhaps that of the moon and the stars, so that the temple could also function as a calendar for the ancient communities. Standing at the major points on the rope (placed earlier between **Wsl** and **Ssl**) and observing the sunrises through the V notch probably allowed the astronomer-priests to identify the dates of the equinoxes and solstices, and apprise the communities of the same. These dates encouraged the people to commence with farming and other significant fertility ceremonies.

Surroundings

A rocky outcrop to the south of the temple forms the quarry from which the stones were extracted and subsequently transported to the temple site. Signs indicating the quarrying of stones from the rock are still discernible. A flat stone platform was discovered here by a few archaeologists of the Archaeological Survey of India, which, according to them, served as a podium, used by the ancients during assemblies and meetings. The presence of iron slag in the fields around the megalithic temple confirms the presence of Asur-type iron-smelting tribes in the area.

Walking past agricultural fields located to the south-east, one arrives at a small hillock where villagers have accumulated some

Buddhist relics and worship the place as 'Tongri Gosain'. One does not know wherefrom these relics were procured or when, but the presence of Buddhist sites adjacent to ancient megalithic complexes being a common feature in Hazaribagh and Chatra districts is indeed testimony to the fact that tribals of this area were once inducted into the Buddhist fold. Half a kilometre to the south-south-east of the megaliths and adjacent to Tongri Gosain once stood a large burial mound created from grits of stone and earth. The monument was about 15 metres in diameter with an almost flat top. Illegal mining for coal had devastated the prehistoric structure at the time of writing this book.

This expanse of sacred land includes not only a megalithic temple, a burial mound, a Buddhist site, and a pond, but also a temple dedicated to Sin Baba. As the name suggests, the temple was used for the worship of Sin Bonga, the prehistoric deity revered by all Proto-Australoid Kolarian tribes in Jharkhand. The shrine, the only one of its kind in the district, comprises about seven small earthen mounds, perhaps representative of hills, and a small rectangular wooden block with pointed nails, on which the *pahan* or priest of this ancient temple, hailing from the Ganju tribe, sat to perform penance.

Archaeological Discoveries

One particular morning a few years ago, I was informed of the collapse of the menhir **M1**. I immediately reported the catastrophe to the deputy commissioner (DC) of Hazaribagh, who promptly instructed the block development officer (BDO) of Barkagaon to arrange the re-installation of the ancient stone under the author's supervision. During the process of raising the menhir, we encountered a burial pitcher barely a foot (0.3 metres) below, in front of where the menhir once stood (Plate 33). The earthen pot, probably buried in accordance to the Sat-Bharwaan ritual, did not seem to be very old. An iron *singie* (Plate 37) fell from the crumbled pot. Digging deeper, we could not find any burial or any other pot below it. The menhir, however, was finally erected with utmost accuracy and returned to its former glory (Plates 35 and 36).

The grounds around the megalith are littered with a large number of potshards. Ploughing around the temple has yielded earthen and stone potteries (Plate 34), various stone tools (Plate 39), and iron implements (Plate 38).

The author had a few of the stone tools dated at the Palaeolithic museum of Dresden, Germany. The dates established in accordance with the patina formation on the tools were startling—the tools dated back to 3000 BC with a few being even older (Imam 2014). These, to my understanding, do not establish the date of the megaliths but authenticate the fact that Stone Age people did inhabit the area around that time.

Based on the estimations of the drift of the tropic of Cancer, the folklore of the various incoming Mundari tribes, and the

---

PLATE 33 *A burial pot is spotted in the process of erection of the fallen menhir.*

PLATE 34 *Earthen and stone pottery from the vicinity of the stone temple of Punkri Burwadih.*

Plate 33

Plate 34

Plate 35

Plate 36

Plate 37

Plate 38

veneration of the omnipresent recumbent Mother Goddess form of Amjhori hill (a primitive belief that perhaps died with the advent of Buddhism and Jainism), my conjecture is that the Punkri Burwadih megalithic astronomical temple could have been built around 1500 BC. However, a proper scientific excavation of the site is necessary to ascertain the antiquity of this megalithic temple. Both the circle on the eastern side of the

---

PLATES 35 AND 36 *Both plates demonstrate the author and his team, comprising Alok Bharti, villagers, and the district administration, erecting MI, the fallen menhir. Credit: Alok Bharti*

PLATE 37 *A villager holds an iron* singie *that had fallen out from a burial pot during the excavation for the raising and cementing of the collapsed menhir. The inset displays another ancient rusted* singie *from a separate megalithic burial.*

PLATE 38 *Iron implements from around the site.*

Plate 39

North–South axis and the oracle stone **B** could contain burials of influential priests of the observatory-shrine.

Local Myths

According to local peasants, the stones evolved naturally and were not erected by humans. The prominence of the shrine spread far and wide, drawing people from distant places to bury the bones of their dead as per the Sat-Bharwaan ritual in the complex, the prevalent belief possibly being that to be buried in such a temple, which was connected to the sacred skies and to the Mother hills, would foster a good rebirth. However, the

PLATE 39 *Various tools yielded while farming in the fields around the megalithic site.*

ritual of Sat-Bharwaan is gradually losing importance with the progressive Hinduisation of such bone-burying ceremonies.

One interesting myth that helped protect the stones from being vandalised is that the villagers once cultivated pulses on the land around the stones in defiance of their ancestor's resolution of practicing no agriculture on this sacred land, which was specifically reserved for the grazing of cattle. The farmers, as I was told, had a dream in which their dead elders rebuked them for such a reprehensible act. Farming was discontinued the following year and the land returned to the cattle, preserving the megaliths in the process.

KATIA MURBEY

Latitude: 24°0'59.76" N | Longitude: 84°58'33.6" E

Accessibility

Katia Murbey is a newly discovered megalithic site, located deep in the heartland of Chatra district. Although the non-tribal Hindu villagers still use the tribal Austric term *hargarhi* for the megaliths, Katia Murbey is in no way a conventional megalithic burial site, like those found in abundance in and around Ranchi. I was taken to the site by one Jitendra Tewary of Pathalgada village; the ancient stone temple is not easy to reach unless guided suitably.

Plate 40

Description

Katia Murbey is in a terrible state of ruin, but, if one notices carefully, the land on which the megalithic temple rests seems to have been artificially raised (Plate 40).

The spread of the megalithic temple cannot be measured because it is difficult to ascertain to what extent the sacred land once stretched. Quite a number of the ancient stones have disappeared and the few that remain stand broken; the fringe areas also reveal parts of standing stones. One may speculate that the sacred site was rectangular.

No other hill except for Dasi seems to be close to the megaliths; therefore, chances are that the menhirs in the complex were

quarried from this hill. However, to learn about the source of the stones an in-depth survey is essential. Beholding the site, one gets an inkling as to how magnificent the site must have once looked, with the display of all the original standing megaliths. The land must have made an overwhelming impression of awe and amazement in the eyes of the rustic tribals. Twelve stones of varied sizes are all that remain of this ancient megalithic temple, out of which a few are already in ruins. The rest of the large stones, as told to us by non-tribal Hindu villagers, for whom these stones have no significance, were towed away by them for routine household purposes.

The top of the tallest stone features a gradient such that the taller side measures 2.032 metres or the standard 80 inches. In other words, these standard measurements must have had some significance that remains unknown to us. One stone with a semicircular crown sits inclined in front of the tall menhir. The rest of the stones have been uprooted, leaving deep depressions on the ground where they once stood.

These cavities on the ground are in a straight line with the remaining, broken stones. This substantiates that the standing menhirs were indeed aligned diagonally with one another in a grid pattern. Examining the land revealed that although most of the stones were indeed placed crossways, a few were

---

PLATE 40 *The astronomical megalithic temple of Katia Murbey.*

DRAWING 4 *The astronomical alignments of the Katia Murbey megaliths towards hills in the horizon to the cardinal points.*

not. The purpose of such 'out of the place' stones could not be well comprehended, but my belief is that these were memorial menhirs randomly planted by later-day megalithic tribes.

Astronomical Orientations

Surveying the megalithic complex reveals that the temple was brilliantly positioned, with a planned design displaying a magnificent hex-sectioning of the circular horizon. Straightforwardly, the ancient temple is located at the intersection point of the alignments of the hills in the rounded horizon.

The first alignment of the temple shows that the menhirs were arranged to face Dasi hill, located due east (Drawing 4) (Plate 41). This is a drift from the normal orientation of menhirs found

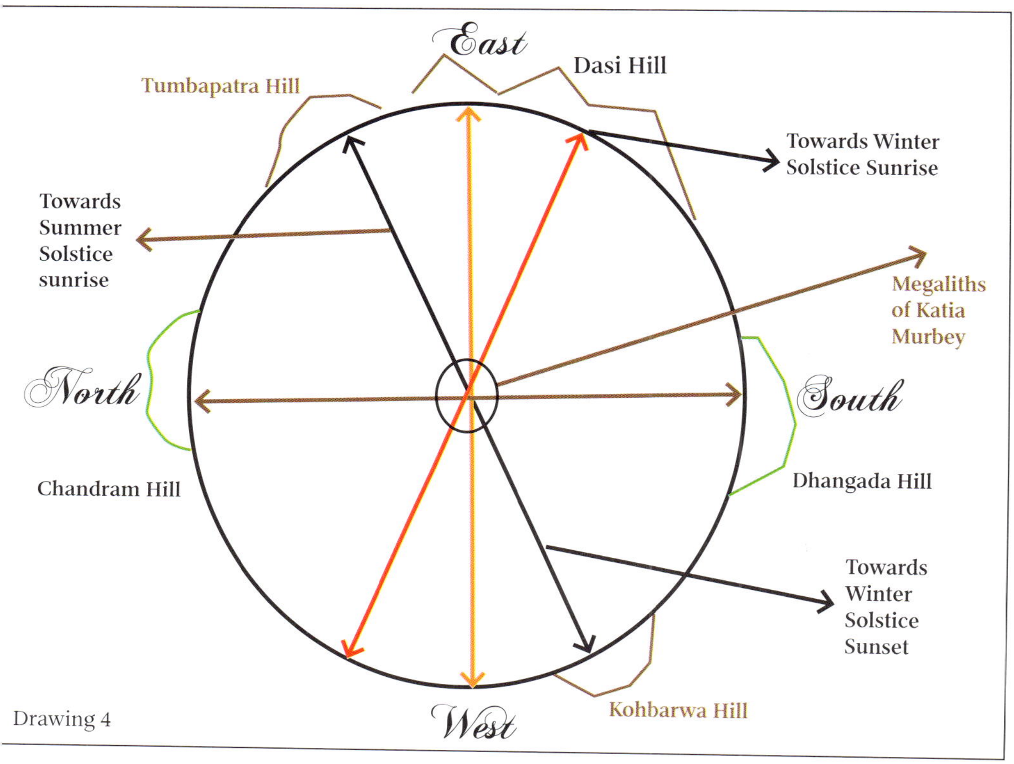

Drawing 4

Plate 41

in northern Jharkhand, where they are made to face the winter solstice sunrise. The megalithic temple is sited exactly between the Chandram and Dhangada hills, located to the site's north and south respectively. The removal of stones has left holes in the ground that align with the remaining stones, which, although oriented to the east, are diagonally connected to the extended range of Dasi hill to the right of the temple, towards the winter solstice sunrise (Drawings 4 and 5) (Plate 42).

The hills for the summer solstice sunset to the left of the temple could not be located. The other diagonal alignments of the menhirs are between the Tumbapatra and Kohbharwa hills—towards the summer solstice sunrise and winter solstice sunset

---

PLATE 41 *The entire site faces Dasi hill located due east. Credit: Alok Bharti*

DRAWING 5 *A diagram of the layout of stones in Katia Murbey, revealing the tentative diagonal alignments towards the sunrises and sets of the summer and the winter solstice respectively that create a grid formation on the ground.*

respectively (Drawings 4 and 5) (Plate 43). Both the right and the left diagonals created by the criss-cross positioning of the stones, bearing their respective alignments towards the Dasi and Tumbapatra and the Kohbharwa hills, create a grid pattern on the ground (Drawing 5).

The diagonals are positioned in parallel rows but are separated from one another at irregular distances. The exact number of stone rows could not be estimated because a good number of

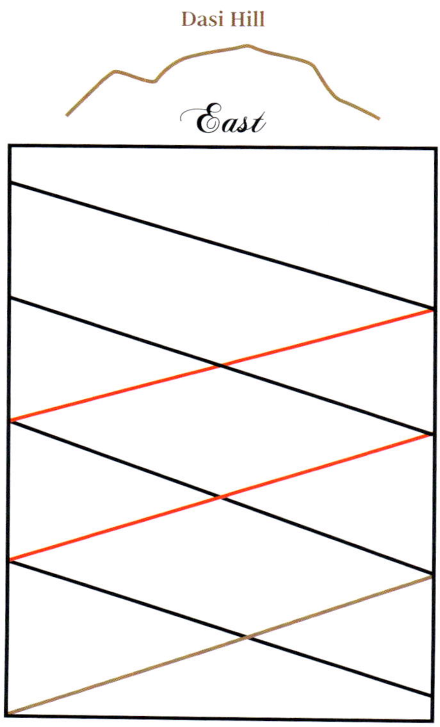

The red lines denote the alignments of the stones in the megalithic site towards the winter solstice sunrise and the summer solstice sunset.

The black lines denote the alignments of the stones in the megalithic site towards the summer solstice sunset and the winter solstice sunset.

Drawing 5

Plate 42

Plate 43

the stones are now missing. Katia Murbey, although relatively smaller, is somewhat identical to the megalithic complex of Vibhuthihalli in Karnataka, where too undressed stones reveal a grid arrangement with diagonal alignments (Allchin 1956, 133).

Purpose

Katia Murbey is indeed very unique; a parallel of this site has yet not been discovered in the state. Although Katia Murbey does reveal applied astronomy, it is not a site analogous to either of Punkri Burwadih or Chano.

At this site, one can certainly observe the sunrises and sunsets of both the equinoxes and solstices. As per my knowledge, burying the bones of the dead and setting a menhir on it in alignment to either of the solstitial sunrises or sunsets is indicative of regeneration, and pertains to the archaic fertility cult.

The name Katia Murbey is a combination of the two Austric Mundari words *'katia',* denoting a rat, and *'murbey',* an old chieftain of a village. Such a name summons the idea that the villages were indeed merged at some point in the past, as in the case of Punkri Burwadih.

The site as per the locals is known as a *hargarhi*, the Austric name for a megalithic burial. Broken potshards that seem relatively

---

PLATES 42 AND 43 *These plates of the ruined megalithic site of Katia Murbey show a few remaining stones that still demonstrate parallel and diagonal alignments towards the sunrises and sets of both the summer and winter solstices Credit: Alok Bharti* new lie scattered all over the site, confirming that Sat-Bharwaan was practised here sometime in the yesteryears. Katia Murbey bears close affinity, architecturally, with Vibhuthihalli, which has not yielded any funerary remains. Whether Katia Murbey, apart from its astronomical orientations, was also created for sepulchral purposes, housing mortal remains of the dead, can be authenticated only by an archaeological excavation. Such an exercise would also enable the estimation of a scientific date for the antiquity of this monument.

BIRBIR

Latitude: 23°59'02.9" N | Longitude: 85°24'51.4" E

Accessibility

Birbir is a village located very close to Hazaribagh. Drive east on the Bagodar state highway and take the right bend from Nutan Nagar towards the village Birbir. The megalith is found on the north-eastern periphery of the village. The drive is about 6 kilometres from town.

Architecture

Birbir is a small but sparkling example of a megalithic complex (Plate 44), surrounded by small hills such as those

Plate 44

of Juljlul, Bawanwey, Kesura, Rola, Adra Hudua, and Kanheri. These megaliths could belong to a period in ancient times when megalithic burials were not granted to every deceased but only to the chief of the community or to the custodian-priest of such temple-shrines. The megalithic temple complex is positioned on sacred elevated ground in the north-eastern part of the village.

The centre of attraction of the complex is an inclined menhir. Even here, the tall stone has been sculpted in accordance to the specific megalithic dimension of about 72 inches or 1.83 metres. One should not be under the impression that the stone is about to fall; the inclines of many menhirs in Jharkhand are deliberate but for reasons yet unknown to us.

About 1.75 metres to the right of the tall stone is a beautifully sculpted human-shaped recumbent stone, which could be the burial cover of the site (Plate 45). The head of the reclining figure is engraved with distinctive eyes, a nose, and a mouth, which, however, could be the handiwork of latter-day village children. Nonetheless, the figure is adorned in female attire, suggesting that the buried person may have been a woman. There are cup-marks on the southern side of the reclining stone. The prostrate

---

PLATE 44 *Birbir megaliths. The long resting stone to the right of the menhir is the human-shaped burial cover. The small triangle points towards the equinox sunrise due east.*

PLATE 45 *The burial cover is a human-shaped stone. The three stones—the burial cover, the menhir, and the triangle (visible behind the menhir)—are placed in a North–South alignment.*

Plate 45

female sculpture demonstrates the prevalent recumbent Mother Goddess cult of the age.

About 2.21 metres to the left of the menhir is a small stone triangle (Plate 44). Triangles, as mentioned before, are typical to Hazaribagh megalithic sites—a characteristic not seen in megaliths elsewhere (Das 2008). To the north of the site is a small *mandapa*. This is a white-coloured, flat-roofed temple dedicated to the Mother Goddess and houses small earthen *pindas* or balls, perhaps symbolic of the hills. A large boulder near the site gives a clue as to the quarry for the megaliths.

Astronomy and Alignments

All the three megaliths in the temple—the tall menhir, the recumbent stone, and the small triangle—are placed on the linear North–South axis (Plates 44 and 45). The feminine burial cover, placed in a North–South orientation, has its head placed towards the north. This is the direction associated with the dead by both Hindus and tribals.

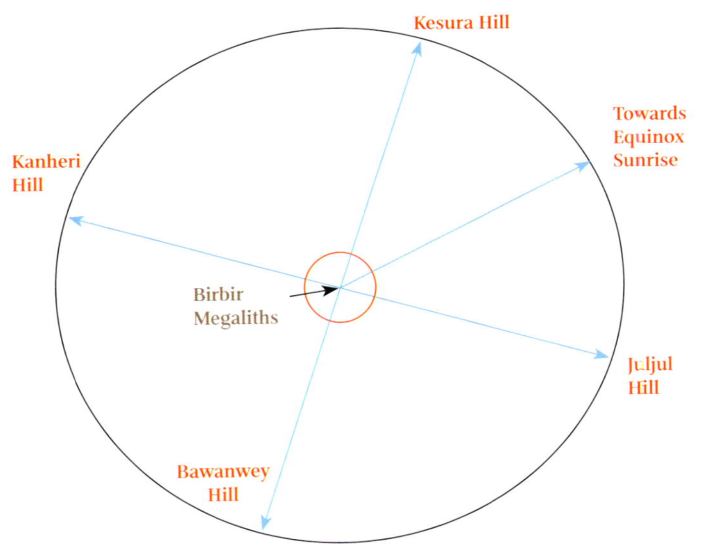

Drawing 6

The 'cross in a circle' is conspicuously perceptible in the complex—the megalithic temple is accurately positioned on the intersection point of the alignments of the Kanheri and Juljul mother hills at 330° N of NW and 150° S of SE respectively, and at 60° E of NE and 240° W of SW of the Kesura and Bawanwey hills respectively (Drawing 6).

The manner in which the ancient megalithic astronomers utilised the small triangle enlightens us of their astronomical insight. The tip of the triangle is accurately aligned to the rising sun on the equinox mornings, a view that is both powerful and mesmerising (Plate 46). The other use of this pointer is manifested in the way the triangle was cut, shaped, and positioned to such exactness that it unerringly 'mirrors' the conical Kesura hill, located 60° E of NE from the megalithic site (Plate 47).

DRAWING 6 *The cross-in-a-circle-type alignment used in the positioning of the Birbir megalithic temple. The monument can be seen to have been placed exactly at the intersection of the alignments of the site to the hills in the horizon.*

PLATE 46 *The small triangle at the site points to the equinox sunrise.*

Plate 47

Standing behind the tall stone facing south, one can conspicuously observe that the menhir snugly 'fits' upon the V notch of Juljul hill (Plate 48). This is an engineered view; the phallic menhir 'fitting' on the V notch, symbolic of the female vulva, is demonstrative of the union of the sexes, vestiges of the fertility cults. A similar display of the phallus 'fitting' in the 'V' of Juljul hill at the Chano megalithic complex has been discussed earlier.

To the north of these three stones is a small horizontal stone slab, on which a cavity that opens towards the Juljul mother hill has been carved (Plate 49). The indentation is unmistakably

---

PLATE 47 *Mirroring. Observe how the triangle mirrors Kesura hill in the horizon.*

PLATE 48 *The menhir is made to snugly 'fit' on the 'V' of the Juljul mother hill, demonstrating copulation in the process.*

PLATE 49 *A female vulva-type indentation has been engraved on a stone adjacent to the tall menhir that faces the Juljul mother hill.*

Plate 48

Plate 49

etched to epitomise the female vulva. Anonymous fertility rites may have been conducted on this relic.

Similar to Hindu cremation grounds, many ancient megalithic burials, too, once featured rivers adjacent to the sites; these rivers flow or once flowed from south to north. In case the river was at a distance from the megalithic site, a deep conduit was dug to enable the water to flow from south to north, on whose banks funerary rites would be performed. A river named Galgal once flowed, from south to north, a few hundred metres to the north of this megalithic complex. The river has now dried up but its channel is still perceptible.

Archaeological Appraisal

Black, red, and black-and-red pottery was collected in situ from the site. The presence of numerous pieces of iron slag gives credence to the claim that the site was once inhabited by Asur-type iron-smelting megalithic tribes.

The recumbent stone, feminine in form, could perhaps comprise the burial of the custodian-priest of this ancient megalithic temple. Whether the site houses any other burials shall only be realised after proper excavation; such an exercise will also help put a date on this ancient astronomical shrine.

OBRA

Latitude: 24°5'48.12" N | Longitude: 85°5'3.84" E

Accessibility

Drive to Pathalgada to arrive at Singhani Chowk, subsequently turning to the south-east. One has to cross Bhuiyan Toli and the serene river Bakulia to arrive at the megaliths.

Architecture

The area manifests an amazing landscape, ringed with hills such as Korambey, Nawadih, Kuba, and Gopipur.

In an area of a few acres are spread about five different megalithic burial sites comprising countless megaliths. One of these megaliths distinctively reveals astronomical implications and would hence form the theme of our treatise hereunder.

Two stones of comparative sizes stand in close proximity and a third lies flat on the ground. The taller inclined menhir, labelled **A1**, is 2.794 metres tall and leans to the right. About 1.28 metres away, the smaller menhir, marked **B1**, having the standard height of 52 inches or 1.32 metres, stands tilted to its left. The third stone that lay fallen on the ground, which we shall call **C**, has a length of 2.38 metres (Plate 50).

At a distance of about 80 metres from the menhirs **A1** and **B1** are two more stones, designated **A2** and **B2** respectively

Plate 50

Plate 51

(Plate 51). **A2** and **B2** are also planted with a tilt, identical to that of **A1** and **B1**. **A2**, with a height of 3.45 metres, is the tallest of the four stones. **B2**, positioned adjacent to **A2**, is in many ways similar to **B1** as they are both inclined to the left and are of almost the same height, i.e. 1.32 metres (Plate 51). The distance between **A2** and **B2** is fascinating as it is almost the same length as that of the fallen menhir **C**.

Astronomy and Alignments

In our survey of Obra, we found that it illustrated a well-planned engineering of alignments that has resulted in a striking design by way of surface architecture at the megalithic site, featuring parallel stones never witnessed elsewhere in the state (Plate 51).

The tall menhir **A1** is tilted towards Korambey hill to the east while **B1** is inclined towards Nawadih hill to the west, in the opposite direction as **A1**. We also found that **B1** is aligned to Kuba at a bearing of 300 degrees NW of W. The fallen menhir **C** lies on the ground adjacent to **B1**; our survey revealed that its tip points due north (Drawing 7). **A2**, as mentioned above, is the tallest stone of the temple and leans to the east towards the V notch of Korambey hill. **B2**, analogous to its kin **B1**, is aligned to a separate peak of Nawadih hill to the west.

PLATE 50 *The three stones of Obra with the newly constructed road in the background.*

PLATE 51 *Obra megaliths. The amazing parallel design of Obra, formulated by a precise positioning of the four menhirs.*

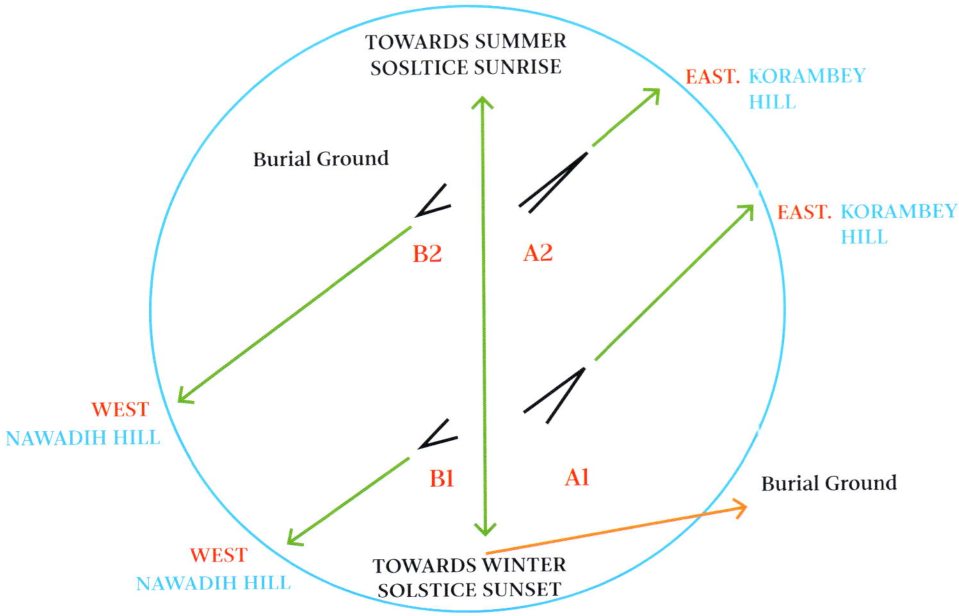

Drawing 7

Standing a little further SW of **A1-B1** and gazing at the megalithic site, one is amazed at the design that the four parallel menhirs manifest. In other words, the arrangement of the menhirs is such that **A1** is positioned parallel to **A2**, and **B1**, tilting opposite to **A1**, is placed parallel to **B2**, which too is positioned leaning opposite to **A2**.

It was no mean feat to create this pattern of parallel stones while also maintaining accurate alignments to the respective peaks and notches of the hills on either side. Why this pattern of parallels was produced by the ancient megalithic engineers,

---

Drawing 7 *The layout of the Obra megalithic temple showing its alignments.*
Plate 52 *Copper artefacts recovered from near the menhirs* A1 *and* A2 *during road construction.*

with such accurate orientation of the four menhirs, cannot be known but is indeed quite a spectacle to behold.

Our examination of the site further revealed that the spaces between **A1** and **B1** and **A2** and **B2** are oriented towards the summer solstice sunrise and winter solstice sunset respectively.

Archaeology

Road construction beside **A1** and **B1** had exposed a few burial pots that yielded only copper remains, including copper slag, copper hooks, and even a copper bell (Plate 52). No iron implements were present inside the pots, giving rise to speculation that iron

Plate 52

Plate 53

may not have been invented at the time. This find of copper objects in Obra presents the possibility that the megaliths here may well belong to the Chalcolithic period.

Adjacent to **A2** and **B2** is a ruined burial ground where one can observe the remains of broken menhirs. Broken potshards and exposed rims of pitchers and pots, many of which reveal charred bones, are omnipresent in this burial ground (Plate 53).

The uncovered pitchers are of different sizes, and are painted red with various patterns inscribed on them. The ground is also

PLATE 53 *An exposed burial pitcher containing charred bones in Obra.*

interspersed with iron slags, suggesting the smelting of iron by iron-smelting Asur tribes such as the Agaria, Birjia, et al.

Purpose

Obra is perplexing as one is at a loss establishing the purpose of the site. If it was meant to serve as a burial for the villagers in the hoary past, then why was such an astronomical positioning used for the four menhirs? In the huge expanse of land around the Obra megalithic site, one can still observe an abundance of standing sepulchral and funerary megaliths, notwithstanding the innumerable ones that have been completely obliterated. It could be that the different megalithic burial sites were for different villages and tribes, and belong to different timelines, but the rationale behind creating such an amazing design is not known.

Excavation of the complex may reveal the mysteries of this temple. My contention is that the burials belong to a later period, and that the four astronomical stones were probably raised during the early Chalcolithic era by anonymous megalithic tribes as their temple.

Plate 54

PREVAILING STATUS OF THE MEGALITHS

Astronomical megaliths, such as the ones examined here, and their tribal makers have the potential to rewrite the ancient history of India.

The monuments discussed in the previous chapters as also the other megaliths in the country are indeed in a pathetic state. Government apathy, indifference of the Archaeological Survey of India and the Jharkhand state archaeological department, along with a burgeoning human populace and its lack of awareness regarding these tribal monuments has led to their disappearance and destruction.

These megalithic temples are indeed testimonies to the prevalence of the knowledge of astronomy and mathematics

---

PLATE 54 *A boundary wall and buildings appear close to the megalithic site of Chano, posing a great threat to the monument.*

among a certain section of megalithic tribes in distant antiquity. The ruination of such astronomical megalithic complexes will undeniably shroud this unknown chapter of India's past; protection and preservation of such temples for posterity is therefore of paramount importance.

The common man, unaware of the significance of these sacred ancient stones, appropriates them for mundane domestic purposes. As discussed earlier, hills form the outer precincts of these open-air megalithic temples, to which the latter are aligned. Most of these hills are being ruthlessly mined today. Unplanned tree plantations and unbridled construction around these ancient megaliths many a time obscure such alignments. Since the alignments of the megalithic temples to the hills are concealed, the sacredness of the temples is thereby lost.

In such a scenario, what rationale for existence would the megalithic temples provide, desolate of their outer walls and their inherent inviolability? Let us then look at each of the megalithic temples already discussed and which face the same predicament of obscurity and annihilation.

CHANO

Numerous buildings have cropped up in close proximity of the prehistoric megalithic complex, which has now become a garbage dump for neighbouring homes. The astronomy of the site is lost forever—the stunning spectacle of the alignments of the stones of the temple towards the winter and summer solstice sunrises and sunsets can no longer be viewed, nor can the alignments to the hills. The common man, having no understanding of these sacred ancient stones, may thus tow them away any day for routine domestic uses.

FURUKA

As the village of Furuka gradually expands towards the lone pillared menhir, the threat of its destruction looms large. The megalith's alignments with the hills to the east is now completely obscured due to the presence of dense foliage and the ever-expanding village.

PUNKRI BURWADIH

The arrival of the National Thermal Power Corporation (NTPC) in the region has jeopardised this ancient megalithic temple. NTPC has embarked on open cast coal mining in the area by procuring land from villagers, who, consequently, have made a beeline for the elevated land around the megaliths. They have now built homes as also dhabas there to cater to the truckers carting coal from the newly opened coal mines.

An electric supply substation of the NTPC has also come up at a little distance from the megaliths; it is not only an eyesore but also hinders any alignments with the hills. Dhabas have also sprouted adjacent to the substation, detracting from both the peace and magnificence of this ancient megalithic site. One particular dhaba that has come up quite near to the megaliths draws a considerable number of large trucks to the field near the megaliths. These are undeniably a menace for this megalithic temple.

The dhabas disturb the amazing 'mirroring' alignment of the three menhirs at the site to the Jugra range of hills. A variety of structures of NTPC are coming up on the hills to which the site is aligned. Indifference of the villagers and the government's apathy towards the temple has only added to its misery.

KATIA MURBEY

This unique megalithic temple was already in a state of ruin when I first visited the site. Nothing much remains of the megaliths to be further destroyed. The large menhirs that once adorned this majestic temple have been hauled away by non-tribal villagers for household purposes. The author has spoken to the non-tribal *mukhiya* or head of the village and implored him to protect whatever remains of this once glorious megalithic site; its fate now rests in his hands.

BIRBIR

The site at Birbir is under the same threat as the one at Chano, with constructions gradually nearing the megalithic complex. The 'mirroring' of the triangular Kesura hill by the triangular stone at the site is already blocked by distant trees and buildings.

OBRA

The astronomical megalithic temple at Obra was already damaged when I first visited the area. A road constructed by the local administration now runs through the site, desecrating the entire temple complex in the process. Ignorance being the greatest bliss, one cannot blame them for this horrendous act as they know nothing about megaliths.

The burial ground was subsequently excavated by villagers in search of buried treasure as broken shards of burial pots and pitchers can be seen scattered throughout the site. The large menhirs that once stood with much grace have also been appropriated by them.

The day, it seems, isn't far away when humankind will lose these amazing astronomical megalithic temples, thereafter to be found only in books and journals.

Plate 55

PARTING THOUGHTS

That prehistoric humankind was indeed knowledgeable in fundamental geometry and observational astronomy is unambiguously apparent from this study of megalithic temples. Site selection for the megalithic temples as also the arrangement of stones inside them serve as definitive evidence of the proficiency of the ancient megalithic engineers in these sciences. The orientations and alignments also reveal the ancients' understanding of the relationship of the landscape and the hills with megaliths (Das 2009, 43–49). Hills, as we know, were sacred entities, deemed to be the breasts or vulva of the Great Goddess. Hills resembling a reclining pregnant woman were revered as recumbent forms of the pregnant Mother Goddess. Such practices and insignia were the accessories of the once prevalent fertility cult.

PLATE 55 *A view of Punkri Burwadih*

Close scrutiny of the archaeoastronomical megalithic complexes covered in this volume presents evidence of adjustments and alterations carried out on the previously laid stones inside them by successive groups of megalithic astronomers. For instance, the menhir **C** of Punkri Burwadih, perhaps initially erected for a separate purpose, was visibly altered and appropriated at a later time. It can be seen to have been knocked down and broken into two parts; the upper portion of the menhir is marked **C2** and is placed nearby while its stump **C1** remains buried in its original position. The sundering of **C** and the positioning of **C2** have been carried out so perfectly that the space between the tip of **C2** and **X** indicates the approximate distance between the equinox and solstice viewing points of **E** and **Ssl** respectively (Drawing 3).

These ancient archaeoastronomical megalithic temples may have been precursors to the Brahmanical, Buddhist, and Jaina temples that came much later, and in which the science of alignments was also effected. The knowledge of megalithic temple architecture, their positioning on sacred land, and the prescribed dimensions for the idols was later dubbed Vastu.

The *Rig Veda* mentions the sun as the greatest inseminator and the same belief was also held by the tribals. For the ancients, the fortunes of the fertility of the soil, their womenfolk, and their cattle depended on the sunrises and sunsets of significant days, such as the equinoxes and solstices, and perhaps even on the erratic movement, position, and the rise of the moon and its solstices—beliefs still prevalent among peasant and tribal societies. This faith originated in the antiquated fertility cult of the Mother Goddess and in which rural India still has firm conviction. Observing the sun rise from specified points in the megaliths perhaps had the custodian-priests know the precise time/date on which the fertility of their women, cattle, and the earth would be enhanced. Alignments were also associated to ancestor worship and regeneration.

As discussed earlier, the sacred hills to which the open-air megalithic temples were aligned formed their outer precincts. Prehistoric pilgrims trekked great distances to arrive at these shrines. These megaliths, to the pilgrims, were Mother temples, where they performed their fertility and funerary rituals. They also venerated the changing forms of the hills, which, to them, were the form of the recumbent pregnant Goddess, as is seen by way of the various alignments and their framing by the menhirs in the megaliths. A few of these fertility/astronomical megalithic temples, such as Chano and Birbir, were also revered for their symbolic union with the Mother hills in the horizon (Plate 48).

These megalithic complexes, which also functioned as astronomical observatories in addition to being burials and fertility temples, gradually changed with the spread of Brahmanism, Buddhism, and Jainism in later times. With the gradual Aryanisation of the land, ideas of the *Vedanga Jyotisha* gradually seeped in. This Aryan science was reliant on *siddhanta* or calculations of the ingress and movements, risings and settings of planets and other celestial bodies. The tribal priests used to study the transits and positions of the sun and the moon by observing them through megalithic observatories, and subsequently pronounced the dates of the fertility and farming rituals of the communities. The advent of Brahmanical astronomy and astrology subsequent to the ancient era halted the dominance of observational and horizon astronomy.

The introduction of Aryan Siddhantic astronomy and astrology along with the gradual spread of Brahmanism, Buddhism, and Jainism in successive times must have put a curb on the further construction of astronomical megaliths by the non-Aryan tribals. Concepts of astronomy and geometry applied in these megaliths were soon forgotten, perhaps as a result of which these monuments ceased to be constructed in the later period. The tribals, too, in times to come, took these astronomical megaliths for ordinary megalithic burials and identified them with ancestor and spirit worship, diverse burial practices, and even tantric rituals.

Our examination of the orientations of several menhirs in and around the Hazaribagh and Ramgarh districts revealed that most of them face the winter solstice sunrise. That various *jang-topa*-type bone-burying ceremonies could be the driving force behind it was discussed in an earlier chapter. The answer to the diagonal alignments of Katia Murbey towards the equinoctial and solstitial sunrises and sunsets may be found in the fertility cult and their ideas on the regeneration of the dead as also their various associated customs. The different megalithic temples in Jharkhand—Chano, Napo, Banadag, Punkri Burwadih, et al.—function as one coherent structure. Each megalithic complex has a unique and remarkable surface architecture, constructed in relation to the landscape. Despite the dissimilarities between them, the basic alignments of cradling, framing, mirroring, etc. are found to be the same.

Modern day tribal megaliths are merely replications of the traditional *sasandiri* or *birdiri*. A modern-day megalithic burial of the various Mundari tribes or the Oraon, therefore, bears no similarity with the astronomical megaliths of Punkri Burwadih, Katia Murbey, Chano, et al. The question that comes to mind is whether it were the ancestors of the present-day Munda, Santal, Asur, or Oraon tribes who arrived at the beginning of the second millennium BC and created the astronomical megaliths of the state.

If yes, then why do these people have no memory of astronomy or geometry, and why their present monuments are devoid of this ancient knowledge? Could it be that such astronomical megaliths were the creations of an unknown tribe, about whom we know nothing and who may have later merged with the other tribes? Or was it a Mongoloid community that migrated to the North East soon after the influx of Proto-Australoid folks in the region? Whoever these people may have been, they brought with them the perennial wisdom of the skies, the hills, and the landscape, as also that of the alignment of sacred stones to the hills.

Relentless Brahmanisation and the advent of Jainism and Buddhism in Jharkhand led the megalithic tribes of the region to adopt these religions. Several tribal customs and funerary practices like the building of mounds and stupas over the dead were absorbed into the Hindu and Buddhist folds respectively. Megalith-making, which was associated with the fertility cult, was discouraged, putting perhaps a near halt to the practice. It could be that when the tribals reverted to the fertility cult, subsequent to the decline of Jainism and Buddhism in the region, megalithism reappeared, but only as a cinerary observance. The knowledge of creating astronomical stone temples was thus lost; astronomy and geometry are palpably absent in later-day megaliths.

These megalithic temples indeed manifest the potential to rewrite the history of India's ancient past. A megalith in Jharkhand is unlike other heritage sites, such as temples or forts, which can stand and thrive on their own. In a megalithic burial-temple, the landscape forms an integral part of it. Each significant stone as also the site itself are aligned to the hills on the horizon, without which a megalithic complex falls into disuse and becomes non-functional.

ACKNOWLEDGEMENTS

I am indeed blessed to have Dr Terence Meaden, the distinguished author and megalith researcher of Oxford University and retired professor of Dalhousie University in Halifax, Canada; Dr Lydia Eckeshawlfe of the Palaeolithic Museum at Dresden in Germany; Bulu Imam, the celebrated researcher, environmentalist, and anthropologist of my hometown Hazaribagh; and Antony Roper Crerar, the noted archaeoastronomer from Wales, as my close associates. With their research, books, and our regular exchanges of information, they have constantly supported, inspired, and guided me in every possible manner during the course of my research and of writing this book. I am grateful to my good friend Dr Meaden, who, taking time out from his hectic schedule, had undertaken the arduous task of performing the first edit of this book.

It would of course be a misdemeanour not to mention Alok Bharti, the eminent anthropologist, Dr Abhishek Mishra, the noted sci-fi writer and geologist, Sujit Mehta, the computer whiz, and Shib Shankar Goswami, the bird photographer, who all, like the Rock of Gibraltar, stood alongside my research all through these years and believed in it. My deepest admiration is for Jitendra Tewary for discovering the amazing megaliths of Katia Murbey and Obra.

To publish a book whose subject matter is scarcely known in this country requires faith and extreme courage. My sincere appreciation for Mr Bikash Niyogi, Ms Tultul Niyogi, and Mr. Nirmal Kanti Bhattacharjee for supporting this endeavour. I was also much privileged to have the young and dynamic Siddhartha Banerjee as the editor of my book. His fastidious approach, dedication, and quest for excellence has indeed given the book a new expression. My heartfelt thanks to him. Thanks are also due to Mr Shashi Bhushan Prasad, the designer of this book, for his judicious placement of images/drawings and the refined layout.

My memo of thanks would not be complete if I do not extend my gratitude to my wife Bubu and son Prantik, who have patiently stood by my side and supported me during the breadth of my research, spanning nearly two decades.

Let me put in writing here that had it not been for you kind souls, this book wouldn't have seen the light of day.

Thank you.

REFERENCES

Allchin, F.R. 1956. 'The Stone Alignments of Southern Hyderabad'. *Man* 56: 133–136.

Babington, J. 1823. 'Description of the Pandoo Coolies in Malabar: With Four Drawings'. *Transactions of the Literary Society of Bombay* 3: 324–330.

Bisht, R.S. 1997. 'Dholavira Excavations: 1990-94'. In *Facets of Indian Civilization: Recent Perspectives* (Essays in Honour of Prof. B.B. Lal), vol. 1, ed. J.P. Joshi, pp. 107–120. New Delhi: Aryan Book Depot.

Chakrabarty, P.B. 1993. 'Monolith Memorials of Meghalaya'. *Himalaya Today* (March–August): 23.

Chakravarty, A.K. 2001. *The Suryasiddhanta: The astronomical principles of the text.* Kolkata: The Asiatic Society.

Commissioner, Department of Archaeology and Museums, Govt of Andhra Pradesh. 2001. 'Excavations at a Megalithic Burial Site—A Menhir at Lingampalli, R.R. District, Andhra Pradesh'. *INTACH Heritage Annual.*

Cope, Julian. 1998. *The Modern Antiquarian: A Pre-millennial Odyssey through Megalithic Britain.* London: Thorsons.

Cousens, Henry. 1926. *The Chalukyan Architecture of the Kanarese Districts,* Archaeological Survey of India, vol. 42, New Imperial Series. Calcutta: Government of India, Central Publication Branch.

Cyriax, T. 1921. 'Ancient Burial-Places: A Suggestion'. *The Archaeological Journal* 78: 205–215.

Dalton, E.T. 1872. *Descriptive Ethnology of Bengal*. Calcutta: Office of the Superintendent of Government Printing.

Damodaran, Vinita. 2002. 'Gender, Forests and Famine in 19th-Century Chotanagpur, India'. *Indian Journal of Gender Studies* 9 (2): 133–163.

Danino, Michel. 2004-05. 'Dholavira's Geometry: A Preliminary Study'. *Puratattva* 35: 76–84.

Das, Subhashis. 2008. 'Some Salient Features of the Surface Architecture of Megaliths of Hazaribagh'. *Puratattva* 38: 181–185.

Das, Subhashis. 2009. *Sacred Stones in Indian Civilization: With Special Reference to Megaliths*. New Delhi: Kaveri Books.

Das, Subhashis. 2010. 'Megaliths of Jharkhand: A New Insight'. *ABACUS* 5 (1).

Das, Subhashis. 2014. *Unknown Civilization of Prehistoric India*. New Delhi: Kaveri Books.

Deglurkar, G.B., and G.P. Lad. 1992. *Megalithic Raipur (1985–1990)*. Pune: Deccan College Post Graduate and Research Institute.

Earis, Irene. 2011. *Sky and Landscape: A Field Guide to Archaeoastronomy*. Leicester, England: Upfront Publishing.

Ghosh, A. 1990. *An Encyclopaedia of Indian Archaeology*. Leyden, New York: E.J. Brill.

Gimbutas, Marija. 1991.*The Civilization of the Goddess: The World of Old Europe*. San Francisco, Calif.: Harper.

Gordon, D.H. 1997. *The Prehistoric Background of Indian Culture*. New Delhi: Munshiram Manoharlal Publishers Pvt Ltd.

Gow, Peter. 1995. 'Land, People, and Paper in Western Amazonia'. In *The Anthropology of Landscape: Perspectives on Place and Space*, ed. Eric Hirsch and Michael O'Hanlon, pp. 43–62. Oxford: Clarendon Press.

Hutton, J.H. 1922. 'The Meaning and Method of the Erection of Monoliths by the Naga Tribes'. *The Journal of the Royal Anthropological Institute of Great Britain and Ireland* 52: 242–249.

Imam, B. 2014. *Antiquarian Remains of Jharkhand*. New Delhi: Aryan Books International.

Koppers, W. 1942. 'Monuments to the Dead of the Bhils and Other Primitive Tribes in Central India: A Contribution to the Study of the Megalith-Problem'. *Annali Lateranensi* 6: 117–206.

Kosambi, D.D. 1962. *Myth and Reality: Studies in the Formation of Indian Culture*. Bombay: Popular Prakashan.

Meaden, G.T. 1992. *Stonehenge: The Secret of the Solstice*. London: Souvenir Press.

Meaden, G.T. 1999. *The Secrets of the Avebury Stones: Britain's Greatest Megalithic Temple*. London: Souvenir Press.

Meaden, G.T. 2016. *Stonehenge, Avebury and Drombeg Stone Circles Deciphered: The archaeological decoding of the core symbolism and meanings planned into these ancient British and Irish monuments*. Saarbrucken, Germany: Lap Lambert Academic Publishing.

Menon, S.M. 2012. *Ancient Stone Riddles: Megaliths of the Indian Subcontinent*. Manipal: Manipal University Press.

Menon, S.M., and M.N. Vahia. 2011. 'Megalithic Astronomy in South India'. In *Mapping the Oriental Sky: Proceedings of the Seventh International Conference on Oriental Astronomy*, ed. T. Nakamura, W. Orchiston, M. Soma, and R. Strom, pp. 21–26. Tokyo: National Astronomical Observatory of Japan.

Moorti, U.S. 1994. *Megalithic Culture of South India: Socio-Economic Perspectives*. Varanasi: Ganga Kaveri Publishing House.

Paddayya, K. 1995. 'The Stone Alignment at Hanamsagar, District Gulbarga, Karnataka'. In *Sri Nagabhinandanam*, ed. L.K. Srinivasan and S. Nagaraju, volume 1, pp. 23–28. Bangalore: Dr. M.S. Nagaraja Rao Felicitation Committee.

Paddayya, K. 1997. 'Colonel Colin Mackenzie and South Indian Megaliths'. *Deccan College Annual Report*: 38–44.

Rao, B.K. Gururaja. 1972. *Megalithic Culture in South India*. Mysore: Prasaranga, University of Mysore.

Rao, N. Kameswara. 2005. 'Aspects of Prehistoric Astronomy in India'. *Bulletin of the Astronomical Society of India* 33: 499–511.

Rao, N. Kameswara, and P. Thakur. 2010. The Astronomical Significance of Megalithic Stone Alignments at Vibhuthihalli in Northern Karnataka. *Journal of Astronomical History and Heritage* 13(1): 74–82.

Rao, N. Kameswara, P. Thakur, and Y. Mallinathpur. 2011. The Astronomical Significance of 'Nilurallu', the Megalithic Stone Alignment at Murardoddi in Andhra Pradesh, India. *Journal of Astronomical History and Heritage* 14(3): 211–220.

Satapatha Brahmana 13.0.1.14; 13.8.1.13

Sinha, S.P. 1997. *Life and Times of Birsa Bhagwan*. Ranchi: Bihar Tribal Research Institute.

Southworth, Franklin C. 2005. *Linguistic Archaeology of South Asia*. London, New York: Routledge-Curzon.

Thapar, B.K., and A.K. Sharma. 1994. *Indian Megaliths in Asian Context*. New Delhi: National Museum Institute.

Van Exem, A. 1982. *The Religious System of the Munda Tribe*. Ranchi: Satya Bharati.

Whitelaw, Ian. 2007. *A Measure of All Things: The Story of Man and Measurement*. New York: Macmillan.

INDEX